WHAT PEOPLE ARE SAYING...

Dr. Mark Miravalle deserves much credit for making the approved apparitions of Itapiranga, Brazil better known. These messages from the 1990s are very important for our times. The Blessed Mother speaks as the Queen of the Rosary and of Peace, and she underscores the importance of the Rosary, Eucharistic adoration, the need for modesty and purity, and devotion to the Most Chaste Heart of St. Joseph.

–Robert L. Fastiggi, Ph.D.

*Professor of Systematic Theology, Sacred Heart Major Seminary, Detroit
Secretary of the International Marian Association*

In this "must read" book, we read about the following apparitions: On October 13, 1917 in Fatima, during the miracle of the sun, Jesus, the Blessed Virgin Mary, and St. Joseph—the Holy Family—appeared and blessed the crowd. In 1994, during the first of the series of apparitions in Itapiranga, Brazil, Jesus, Mary, and Joseph also appeared, and Jesus later called for the consecration of the church and of the world to the Most Chaste Heart of St. Joseph, who will continue to defend and protect us in this anti-family and apocalyptic era.

–Professor Courtenay Bartholomew

*Emeritus Professor of Medicine of the University of the West Indies
in Trinidad and Tobago. He is the author of six books on Mariology
and a contributor to many Marian conferences worldwide.*

The Three Hearts — Church Approved Apparitions from the Amazon Jungle, is a perfectly-timed work about the apparitions in Itapiranga, Brazil, and contains many messages that are meant for the world at large. Dr. Mark Miravalle, an expert in Mariology and a prolific author, doesn't simply glean some of the messages for us, but he went right to the visionary himself, Edson Glauber, asking him "to select what he considered to be the 'heart' of the message of Itapiranga." Like a master weaver, he highlights the patterns of the messages to help bring together the necessary detailed picture.

–Joe Pronechen
Correspondent, National Catholic Register

Written in an accessible style with profound theological insight, Miravalle's *The Three Hearts* is the first English-language book to point the spotlight on the little-known, but greatly significant, Church-approved and ongoing messages of the apparitions at Itapiranga. These messages are filled with an urgent call to conversion and reason for great hope.

–Michael O'Neill
Author of Exploring the Miraculous
Creator of MiracleHunter.com and host of
The Miracle Hunter *on Relevant Radio*

THE THREE HEARTS

Church Approved Apparitions
from the Amazon Jungle

DR. MARK MIRAVALLE

FAITH & FAMILY
PUBLICATIONS

Published By:
Faith & Family Publications
PO Box 365
Downingtown, PA 19335

www.faithandfamily.pub
info@faithandfamily.pub

ISBN: 978-0-692-95005-0

Printed in the United States of America

CONTENTS

CHAPTER I

QUEEN OF THE ROSARY
AND OF PEACE

F rom the remote regions of the Amazon Jungle, the Mother of God has revealed an extraordinarily critical message for Brazil, for the Church, for the world, and even, it made be said, for the future of humanity. The Mother of Jesus has, moreover, not come alone. She is accompanied by her Divine Son and her virginal husband, in what will comprise a historic new understanding of the Holy Family and the powerful efficacy of devotion to "The Three Hearts."

The intention of this little work is to *introduce you* to *Itapiranga* and the fundamental message of the *Queen of the Rosary and of Peace*. This small text seeks to provide you with the *kerygma* or "gospel" of Itapiranga, and not its *didache* or extended teachings (which, in its own right, this sublime body of supernatural messages deeply merits). In fact, I will strive to keep my commentary to a bare minimum (save for a succinct theological introduction to the new concept of devotion to the "Heart" of St. Joseph, Chapter 4) so as to facilitate, rather than to obstruct, the personal meeting of your heart with the Heart of the Madonna of Itapiranga, and as well—necessarily— your heart's encounter with the other Two Hearts intimately and inseparably conjoined with Her Immaculate Heart.

We begin with the facts of history and chronology.

In the spring of 1994, Edson Glauber (born October 27, 1972) was a twenty-two year old Brazilian college student who was studying Science of Communication Radio and TV in the major city of Manaus, some 5 hours away by car from his family's native town of "Itapiranga." Itapiranga is situated in the environs of the great and majestic Amazon Jungle. In her first apparition, Our Lady appeared to his mother Maria do Carmo on May 2, 1994. The Blessed Virgin Mary soon would identify herself as the "Queen of the Rosary and of Peace." During one of Our Lady's earliest apparitions, on September 4, 1994, she conveys to Edson (while back in Itapiranga) the following message:

> *I am the Queen of Peace! Pray for the youth, because they have much need for your prayers to guide them in their lives.*

> *Even in this small town, simple and humble, the people are turning too much to material things, particularly money. Pray much. I need your prayers so that my plans can be realized. Pray the Rosary! Satan is taking many souls of my children into the darkness. This is why you need to pray much to save them. My children still do not understand the meaning of how I want to realize a feast day in my honor: in prayer and silence.*

On December 25, 1996, Edson reports a vision where he sees the three Hearts of Jesus, Mary, and Joseph, all three gathered on the same horizontal level. Our Lady had roses around her Heart and a sword that pieced it, the Heart of St. Joseph had 12 white lilies with the cross and wounds in the shape of an "M", and the Heart of Jesus had

a crown of thorns. Mary's heart radiated light to the Heart of St. Joseph, the small Child Jesus heart, who was in the arms of St. Joseph radiated light into St. Joseph's Heart, and St. Joseph's heart radiated light to the world (reaching the ground). The Heart of Jesus, on the right side of the image, was deliberately aligned at the same height as the Heart of St. Joseph and of Our Lady's heart, so that the image particularly emphasized the *unity* of the three Hearts rather than a priority of one heart over the others.

Maria do Carmo would also receive apparitions and locutions from Jesus, Mary and Joseph. When questioned by Edson as to why Our Lady and Jesus were both appearing, Our Lady responded: *"Because I want to show all my children all over the world the love of a mother that I have for my Son, Jesus, and the love of a Son that Jesus has for me. For this, I chose to appear as mother and Son."* This, perhaps, also bears significance as to why this heavenly Mother and Son chose to appear to an earthly mother and son combination.

Maria's first locution to the world on May 11, 1994 came from Jesus. As Our Lord woke her from sleep, Edson's mother felt "a force" pull her from her bed, and Jesus instructed her to write down a message being relayed to Maria. At this point, Maria was not sure who was speaking to her, but nonetheless got up and grabbed a piece of paper which was wrapping a loaf of bread, and wrote the message down as instructed. Jesus gave her the following message on the sinful nature of adultery, along with a series of succinct but inspired pastoral directives concerning the present confusion on marriage, divorce, remarriage, and cohabitation (which, in a few inspired lines, summarizes the heart of the teachings of the Church's teaching on the subject as contained in the recent document of Pope Francis, *Amoris Laetitia*):

Adultery is a serious sin, but it can be forgiven with a good confession and total repentance. Teach. You know how to make a good confession. Do not be afraid or ashamed of the priest. If the priest forgives, so do I. If he does not forgive, neither do I. Whoever is married and is now separated should again be reconciled if they still love each other—with forgiveness and sincerity!

Whoever is married and is estranged, and is living with another person who is not their spouse should separate and live as friends in the same house. They can no longer live as husband and wife. If one of them is free to marry and have a conjugal life, this person should then get married. One can simply not commit adultery!

Later, Maria recalled that she had been pondering these questions, as she was concerned with some of her family's living situations and wondered how best to speak to them about it.

Soon after, Our Lady appeared and revealed this message to Maria: *"My army is being built. One by one, I am knocking at your hearts, opening and preparing them for My Son, Jesus. Open up your hearts now, because my Son is already coming to stay with you!"* Maria saw a vision of a river of crystal clear water, and understood it to represent the grace that Jesus wants to grant to the Amazonas region and to the entire world through these formidable contemporary apparitions.

Another early message given by Our Lady to Maria directed her to "turn off the television" and "pray and do penance" along with the call to pray the entire four mysteries of the Rosary daily when possible:

Turn your television off. Do not watch TV. There is nothing worthy to be seen on television nowadays. Pray constantly. Pray the rosary, for the world needs a great deal of prayer. Pray and do penance. Pray the Rosary every day, preferably on your knees, during one week. You need to do penance for your sins. You need to hear my messages more.

Another initial message, this time from Jesus to Edson's mother, called for obedience to Our Lady and the practice of works of mercy to those in most need:

Obey My Mother. Do whatever She asks you to do. Do not remain idle. You have become too much inert. Take action. You have to be humble, caring, kind, loving and obedient. Go visit the imprisoned, the sick at the hospitals, the abandoned children, the neglected elders and widows. Do penances. You know you have to be vigilant.

This message was immediately followed by another very important message:

Here Jesus expressed His wishes for us to do acts of mercy, so that we too may achieve mercy. We cannot remain indifferent to sufferings of our brothers who suffer most. It is Jesus who is asking this of each one of us.

On June 22, 1994, while still in Manaus, Maria received a vision of Our Lady with Jesus and St. Michael the Archangel, all of whom were appearing in the village of Itapiranga, at a specific location belonging to Edson's father. Our Lady stated to Maria:

I request that you build a little chapel at this place, using straw for now. Here in the state of Amazonas, I have chosen the city of Itapiranga during the end of times. In other locations, where I am seen and where I have been giving my messages, my apparitions are to be concluded. And then in Itapiranga, they will begin.

Soon after, the Mother of Jesus appeared again to Maria and conveyed this message, which speaks about the future possibilities of Itapiranga becoming as historic as what happened in Fatima:

My Son and I have chosen this family, your family, to summon the people to pray more, here in Manaus and in Itapiranga.

The city of Itapiranga will be a holy city if all of you pray! What happened in Fatima in 1917 may also happen here. The Enemy wants to reign in this town, but he will not succeed.

On July 15, 2014, Our Lady conveys to Maria a communication regarding the quintessential role of the woman in the family and in the home:

The woman is the one responsible for everything that happens within her house or her family. She is responsible for the conversion of her children, of her husband, and afterwards, for the conversion of her relatives and close kin. As she was able to win his heart in order to date and marry her, in like manner she should lead him to daily prayer. Not only for a single day, but for as long as she lives. Don't you feed yourself every day? Likewise, you should also do with prayer.

As one who labors has the right to eat, the one who does not labor does not eat either. So it is with salvation. Whoever prays will be saved, but the one who does not, will not be saved. Salvation depends on each person, but the [spiritual] help of a woman, or of a mother or friend is welcomed. I want the conversion of all people, all of them!

This warning is for every person from the same household or family. Thus all of them will convert. Announce it. Do not remain inert. Cheer up. Take action. Pray the Rosary of love every day and all day long.

On the feast of St. Teresa of Avila (October 15, 1994), Our Lady reveals to Edson her longest message since the heavenly communications began. She calls for reparation for sin, a renewal of love in hearts, and the directive for all people to *"consecrate yourselves every day to the Immaculate Heart and the Sacred Heart"*:

Would you like to sacrifice for the remission of your sins? Love me. Let your love be your penance. My son, write down my message of love for my other children: I am the Mother of God and I come to you because this is my Son Jesus' desire! The Church needs prayers without ceasing. Pray for my children priests; they need your prayers.

Love has to sprout from the bottom of your hearts. Love each other as my Son Jesus loves you. Pray the holy Rosary with love, with your heart. Meditate upon the sacred mysteries of the Rosary. My Son Jesus always waits for you with open arms. He deeply desires to help you overcome every trouble found in your earthly journey. Call on Him, and He shall help you. He is your greatest friend!

I am the Mother of the Church and all of you are my children. Trust and seek refuge in the Sacred Heart of Jesus and in My Immaculate Heart. Love shall reign in your hearts! Write it down [to them]: so that they can believe as if they had seen Me. Do not be burdened by affliction. Peace shall reign in your hearts, the peace that comes from God!

My Children, I cannot answer all your inquiries, for I obey primarily the will of the One who has sent Me, to whom I submit Myself humbly. I cannot interfere in the plans that God has set for each one of you. I can only indicate the means and the way to which each one of you may fulfill the will of the Lord: through prayer, penance, sacrifices, the Word of God, and the Eucharist. Always pray the Rosary and you will have the power to overcome your tribulations. Do not wait for answers because you will not have them. Read the Bible. There you shall find your answers. Nonetheless, I tell you: convert. Change your lives. Follow my instructions and you will receive abundant divine grace.

Prayer shall be for you a reason for joy, of an encounter with God. If you have not achieved this goal, you will hardly ever have peace in your hearts. You need to strive every day to develop a "spirit of prayer". I cannot perform this for you, because the task to improve yourselves each day belongs to you. Only thus shall you be able to decide for God.

Consecrate yourselves every day to our Sacred Hearts, Mine and My Son Jesus', and offer us your preoccupations, jobs, trials and tribulations, for the conversion of souls of the poor sinners. Remain watchful! Pray that you do not fall into temptation, for the Enemy tries at all cost to lead each one of you to his dark and mortal path. Pray without ceasing so that you may overcome him. Guard yourselves with the Rosary and the Word of God. Once more, I beseech you that love may reign in your hearts! With love, you may perform great things and wonders in your lives. My children, live in love! Always keep your hearts open to My Son, Jesus. Jesus is deeply saddened by the lack of love in humanity. For that reason, love, love, love. Let love be your greatest goal. The more you love, the more you will be purified day after day.

My heart and my Son Jesus´ are united in love. Likewise, you need to be united in constant love with your heavenly Father and with your neighbor. Live my messages. Listen to my pleas, so that you may experience joy while still on this earth, and later be joyful in the heavenly glory. I love you and I bless all of you in the name of the Father, the Son, and the Holy Spirit. Amen. Praise be to Our Lord Jesus Christ!

Our Lady, at this moment, took a book in her hands and showing it to my mother said:

This is the book of Life (The Bible). Read it every day. Many are still not reading it. Start from here. Be an example to others. Make an effort.

An extremely serious message from the Mother of God was revealed on October 29, 1994, concerning "a great chastisement" which is "very soon" and "coming for the whole world." Our Lady calls for confession, conversion, forgiveness, and the imperative to "pray the Rosary every day, and for peace in Brazil":

Pray, pray, and pray. Pray unceasingly! God, Our Lord, is very sad because of your sins. My heart is covered with thorns and pierced by a sword of pain because of your sins. Love each other.

Do not keep hatred and resentment in your hearts. Confess your sins so that you will be free from Satan's hands. The devil is leading many of My children's souls to hell. I need all of you to help me save these souls.

You need to be light for all of these children of Mine. Deny yourselves. Set an example. Do not disregard My Motherly supplications, who suffers for what is about to happen to you. A great chastisement is coming for the whole world, and it is already at hand! Many will suffer if there is no conversion; so, pray the Rosary every day for Brazil and for the peace of the whole world.

Two days later, on October 31st, (global celebration of Halloween), Our Lady appeared with tears of blood, and in her final major message of this first year of apparitions, conveyed this sorrowful message to Maria, along with the following ejaculatory prayer of intercession and reparation for the "many souls taking the path to Hell":

My Son and I are crying tears of blood! There are many souls taking the path to hell. Pray, pray, pray! Pray at the cenacle this ejaculatory prayer that you shall now learn:

Beloved Father, I love Thee. Beloved Mother, I love Thee. Beloved Father and Beloved Mother I love Thee, I love Thee, I love Thee!

… Three times with your heart.

From 1994 to 1998, profound apparitions and locutions from Jesus, Mary, and Joseph (as well as occasionally from St. Michael and St. Gabriel the Archangels) would continue for both Edson and his mother. On May 2, 1998, the Queen of the Rosary and of Peace made her last public appearance at Itapiranga, stating that she had completed the heavenly task of conveying to the people what she had intended to reveal there. It was now time, Our Lady indicated, to put her teachings into practice.

From 1998 through 2000, Edson continued to have apparitions in other parts of Brazil, as well as in Italy, especially during prayer gatherings with young people. Since 2001, Our Lady frequently appears to Edson on Saturdays during prayer meetings which take place in Edson's home. She has, moreover, specifically requested a Christian evangelization directed in a distinct way towards the youth. She has also requested the construction of a simple chapel for pilgrims, as well as the institution of a soup kitchen in Itapiranga for needy children.

The Queen of the Rosary has likewise directed that the water which flows from the place of apparitions in Itapiranga be brought to the sick for healing. A great number of miraculous healings have been reported, positively assessed by doctors, and forwarded to the Apostolic Prefecture of the Archdiocese of Itacoatiara.

The Itapiranga apparitions and their subsequent messages have received a legitimate form of Church approval, as manifested in a "Decree of Public Worship," issued by the local bishop, Dom Carillo Gritti, Bishop of Itacoatiara on January 31, 2010. In this decree of veneration, Bishop Gritti grants ecclesiastical approval for the faithful to pilgrimage and publicly venerate at the "Sanctuary of the Queen of the Rosary and of Peace." As the document states: "This Order of Worship seeks to promote the spiritual life of God's people arriving here to honor the apparitions of Our Lady, the devotion of which originated in this place."

Note that Bishop Gritti not only granted ecclesiastical approval for general public devotion at the location, but specifies devotion stemming directly from the apparitions themselves. This statement from the local bishop clearly indicates a form of Church approval, the authority of which, as the Vatican Congregation for the Doctrine of the Faith confirms, rests in the first instance with the judgment of the local bishop.

Moreover, in a subsequent official document from the local bishop referring to the May 2, 2010 commencement of a Sanctuary for the "Three Sacred Hearts," Bishop Gritti repeatedly cites in positive affirmation the "manifestations" of "Our Lady" to the visionary Edson, whom the bishop refers to as the sincere and devout "bearer of visions and messages worthy of being appreciated." The expression "visions and messages worthy of being appreciated" found in an official document from the local bishop clearly manifests an expression of Church approval.

In the same document, Bishop Gritti states that his launching of the New Sanctuary is in direct response to the call of the Virgin during her various manifestations, for devotion to the "Three Sacred Hearts."

Being that in the various manifestations, the Virgin has called for a devotion to the Three Sacred Hearts of Jesus, Mary, and Joseph, on May 2, 2010, we launched the first stone for a new Sanctuary in honor of the three Sacred Hearts in the certainty that one day it will be the place of many pilgrimages (see Appendix Two for full text).

This statement by Bishop Gritti shows, beyond a shadow of a doubt, not only his personal belief in the supernatural character of the apparitions of Itapiranga, but also his public Church approval, which led him to establish a diocesan approved Sanctuary to the Three Hearts, based on the directives of the Queen of the Rosary and of Peace.

In sum, beyond a shadow of a doubt, the apparitions of Itapiranga have received a form of Church approval.

The first years of a major Marian apparition bear a particular importance in the overall event, for these messages tend to lay the groundwork and foundation for the overall heavenly message and subsequent experience of grace and conversion. The first years of the Itapiranga event will therefore be the particular (though not exclusive) focus of our study. I personally requested the visionary, Edson Glauber, to select what he considered to be the "heart" of the message of Itapiranga. Edson consequently sent me a selection of messages from 1994, 1995, 1996, 1997, and as well as messages of 2001. This brief study will therefore seek to primarily focus on these particular messages, which indeed lay the proper foundation for the overall Itapiranga experience.

As we saw, 1994 provided a genesis of the message and phenomena from the Queen of the Rosary and of Peace, as well as from Our Lord Jesus Himself. This next year of 1995 will see a greater frequency and quality of messages, some new and critically important themes, as well as the beginnings of a populous following as manifested in a positive and generous *vox populi,* or "voice of the people," response to this supernatural message from the "Three Hearts" to our own human hearts.

CHAPTER II

ITAPIRANGA CONTINUES

I n the year 1995, the Itapiranga apparitions will see nearly five times the messages revealed in 1994. Along with a continuation of themes such as the need to "pray the Rosary daily" and "turn off your television," Jesus and Our Lady will reveal an entirely new body of developmental messages in this heavenly call from the Amazonas. These new themes will include the call for "family rosary," Our Lady's self-identification as "Queen of the Youth," the imperative to frequently "go to confession," the confirmation that the "true Church is the Roman Catholic Apostolic Church", and, on a most serious note, that a "torrent of chastisements" are soon approaching.

What follows constitute some of the most important messages from the decisive 1995 second year of Itapiranga apparitions. (Please note: the complete body of 1995 messages can be found in Chapter 6).

The Queen of the Rosary and of Peace begins 1995 with a sacramental call for Eucharistic Adoration, Confession, and for intercessory prayer for the fulfillment of her plan for Itapiranga (January 3rd):

Pray that all my plans will succeed.

Visit my Son Jesus in the Blessed Sacrament, because He feels forsaken with no one to visit Him. Confess your sins and ask God for forgiveness for your daily offenses. May My child Jesus bless you and grant you His peace. Pray and fast.

Beloved children, pray that all my plans come true in this city and in the entire world as soon as possible. I am the Immaculate Conception. Satan is furious to see that you are praying, but fear not. I will protect you and keep you all under my mantle.

In a region formerly dominated by its predominant Catholic presence but now divided into numerously growing Christian denominations (and to new age and the occult practices), Our Lady re-affirms the truth that the Catholic Church is the one "true Church" founded by Jesus Christ (January 10, 1995):

Beloved children, there is only One God and one Faith. Do not be deceived by the snares and false religions instituted by Satan. The true Church founded by My Son, Jesus Christ, which is worthy of faith, is the Roman Catholic Apostolic Church, which has in the holy Father the representative of My Son Jesus ...Obey the Church and follow its teachings with living faith and you shall be saved.

It is undeniable that one of the key pillars of the Itapiranga message is a strong and recurring mandate to daily pray the Rosary. On January 13, 1995, we see not only the call for family rosary, but also the directive to for each individual to "carry your own Rosary beads" on their persons:

Pray the Rosary every day. May every family pray the Rosary and each one of my children carry his own. This weapon defends them from the Evil One. Use it daily. Carry it with you wherever you go. Pray the Rosary, dear children. Listen to My petitions. I bless all of you with the blessings of joy, so that you will pray to the Lord with great fervor.

Several messages of 1995 speak of the hesitancy on the part of some to accept the Itapiranga apparitions as authentic. On January 15, 1995, Our Lady pleads that her Immaculate Heart not be wounded by ongoing doubts, but rather to respond with greater prayer, as many souls are presently in risk of eternal damnation:

Dear children, I am your Mother; hence, don't harm my Immaculate Heart with your doubts. Pray with your hearts, little children. Help me, dear children; do penance for sinners, because many souls are at risk of eternal damnation, since they have no one to pray and make sacrifices for them. Pray the holy Rosary every day for your brethren who find themselves in the path of sin, and for yourselves.

Little children, I beseech you: listen and live what I am asking from each of you, otherwise many souls may be cast down into hell. My children, I still see many sins within you; thus, confess your sins. Cleanse your souls, little children. Go to Holy Mass with a purified heart. Prepare yourselves in advance with prayers and contrite souls so that you be prepared to receive my Son, Jesus, who is in the Holy Eucharist.

Little children, abandon the vices of this world. Renounce in particular, smoking, alcohol, and television programs. Know that it is Jesus who is requesting this. And I, as His humble servant, deliver to you His message. May the mothers instruct their children to pray the holy Rosary and that each family pray it united. I leave you an urgent and worrying message: convert yourselves as soon as possible. You do not know what God will send to the world if there is no conversion.

On January 23, 1995, Our Lady underscores the importance of Holy Mass and Eucharistic Adoration, along with the imperative for sacramental Confession before receiving Communion after grave sin:

Renounce Satan by praying the Rosary and attending to Mass in order to belong entirely to Jesus. Jesus waits for you in the Eucharist with an immeasurable love. Come to the Holy Mass to belong to Him totally. Confess your sins. Do not receive My Son, Jesus, if you are in grave sin. First cleanse yourselves through holy confession. There is a risk of eternal damnation for many, when they live indifferently in sin without seeking confession as they should. Be sincere with My Son Jesus Christ, who poured out all of His Blood and gave His Life for your salvation.

As is oftentimes the precedent in Marian apparitions, St. Michael the Archangel delivers strong messages that convey the legitimate justice of God, and the subsequent call for increased prayer, sacrifice, and reparation, in order to atone and mitigate the full impact of divine justice (February, 1995):

Today I come to bring a very important message directly from the Most Blessed Virgin Mary, Mother of God. Do penance and make sacrifices to redeem the souls of poor sinners. Push yourselves to pray the Rosary and pray it especially for peace in the entire world, because the world is urgently in need of it.

The most Holy Virgin has come to the world on many occasions during these recent times to call you to repentance and to return to the Lord. However, She has not been heard as She should because of men's ingratitude. Do not reject the messages that the Mother of God herself has been conveying to you for a while now. Pay heed to them and act upon them as soon as possible, for the present times are very urgent and concerning.

The world has completely forsaken the Lord and despises Him every moment. How much suffering has been inflicted to the most Holy Virgin. She sheds tears of blood, supplicating the Father's mercy to this perverse and sinful world. She asks the Father to pour His peace and His love upon humanity, so that punishment might be avoided.

You do not know what may be coming for this unfortunate sinful humanity. Pray, asking My powerful protection and I promise to pray to the Lord for each one of you. Pray asking peace for the world. Visit the most Holy Sacrament of the altar, devoting hours of reparation to Our Lord, who so intensely suffers due to blasphemies, ingratitude, and disrespect coming from mankind at each moment. Pray, children of the Lord, pray!

And again from St. Michael:

Son of the Lord, here is my message for today, sent directly from the Lord and from the Most Holy Virgin.

You must make sacrifices and penances for the conversion of poor sinners. Visit the Blessed Sacrament of the altar frequently to make reparation to Jesus in the Eucharist. He is enduring constant transgressions from sinners, especially now that, in your country, carnival holiday is approaching. Therefore, I, St. Michael, as commanded by God, invite you to pray for amendment, committing every deed done throughout from day to day, in atonement and penitence for the conversion of the ungrateful sinners. Everything is worth doing when it is done and delivered with love to our God and our Lord Jesus Christ. The Most Holy Virgin insistently asks her beloved children to publicly worship Her Son in the Blessed Sacrament, to keep vigils and do acts of reparation to the Lord, and ask Jesus Christ to pour the grace from His Mercy over all of you, here in this city, in the state of Amazonas, and especially in Brazil and the entire world, so that His plans be fulfilled as soon as possible.

Pray the Rosary every day, especially the ones from the tears of blood from the Blessed Virgin Mary; the tears poured out by the Holy Virgin are postponing the punishment that might come against humanity.

Jesus refuses nothing because of the tears of His Most Blessed Mother. The Blessed Virgin has daily offered the merits of Her Son Jesus Christ to the Father, along with Her tears of blood, so that abundant blessings and graces of conversion may be bestowed upon the world, especially to those most hardened by sin. The current times are urgent and very critical; still, you have paid little attention to the ones chosen by the Holy Virgin to spread these messages. Return, children of God, return. The Father will not hesitate to deliver His Divine anger over the ones who have rejected Him. Those who reject Him will remain with Satan and his followers. I, St. Michael, the Archangel, along with St. Gabriel and St. Raphael, and all the angels, bless you: in the name of the Father, the Son, and the Holy Spirit. Amen.

Several messages of 1995 identify Our Lady's special love and concern for the *youth of today*, as well as the grave need for conversion among many young people. On February 22, 1995, the "Queen of the Youth" speaks to her children:

I am the Queen of the Youth, the Mother of God, and here from Itapiranga, I make a call to all young people, as I have never made before: return to My Son Jesus. He loves you. Itapiranga is and shall ever be a call for deep conversion of the young people. I am your Heavenly Mother and I do not want any of you to be lost forever on the road to hell. For this reason I come to your aid, to teach you and show you the path of Salvation, the road that leads to God.

As St. Maximilian Kolbe teaches, the Holy Spirit (by divine disposition and not through necessity) acts only through Mary, his Immaculate human spouse. It is therefore no wonder that in her March 16, 1995 message, Our Lady instructs humanity to pray to the Holy Spirit, her divine Spouse, and to request his multiform gifts:

Pray intensely to the Divine Holy Spirit. Do not abandon the One who is your Light, your true Wisdom and your Life. Pray and ask the gifts of the Holy Spirit for yourselves and for your brethren. If you knew what the Holy Spirit has intended for each one of you, you would pray to Him more so that He would change your lives. The Holy Spirit is entirely love and tenderness. May the

Holy Spirit descend upon each one of you and give you His peace, strength, and comfort. May He overshadow you and pour Himself out unto you in grace and abundance. Pray little ones, pray. I am the Virgin of Grace. Pray and I will ask and obtain from the Lord many blessings for each one of you.

In this March 16th message, Jesus asks the visionary Edson for his cooperation with Him in a spirit of love so that this great work can reach its desired fruition. He also reiterates that the union of the Two Hearts means that whoever obeys His Mother will, in that very act, be obeying Jesus:

I expect a little aid and love from you. Will you, by the way, respond to My request? Will you listen to my appeal? O little children, how I pity this poor sinful humankind! How deaf are you humans to My heavenly requests! Don't fall asleep, don't stop. Pray, pray, pray. Don't you know that you are witnessing the great times preceding My return to your midst? Be prepared because the time is imminent. For that reason, I have sent you many signs, and the most beautiful one is my Heavenly Mother, who is instructing you to live in My paths and teachings. Listen to Her. Whoever listens to My Mother, listens to Me. Whoever obeys My Mother, obeys Me. The world is deaf and does not listen. Why? Why do they reject and close their eyes and ears to what we ask? Are you weary, my children? Don't you know the time is very urgent? Pray and be on guard so that you do not fall into temptation. I, the Lord, bless you all.

On May 11, 1995, Jesus stresses to Edson the importance of a good confession in response to the unspoken, internal question of one attending young person at a prayer meeting:

To open your hearts you need a good and holy confession.

Love: Love each other as I love you. Open up your hearts. Learn to listen to Me when I speak to your heart. To open up your hearts you need a good and holy confession. Do not accumulate sins in your hearts. Go to confession.

Edson: On that day, I was praying with a youth group in a house in Itapiranga. One of the young people asked during the apparition (to himself): "How can I open my heart? How does one open his heart?" For that reason Jesus answered in that message: *"To open up your hearts you need a good and holy confession. Do not accumulate sins in your hearts. Go to confession."*

July 17, 1995 brought a rare message from St. Gabriel the Archangel. He asked for reparation to the Sacred and Immaculate Hearts of Jesus and Mary, who suffer so much due to the ubiquitous sins throughout the world—sins which are committed directly against their Two Most Precious Hearts:

Son of the Lord, pray, pray, and pray. Make reparations to the offenses against the Sacred Heart of Jesus and the Immaculate Heart of Mary. The hearts of Jesus and Mary are very sorrowful because of the sins committed around the whole world. Comfort Jesus through reparation for the countless sins perpetrated against His Blessed Mother and He Himself. The holy Hearts of Our Lord Jesus Christ and our Most Blessed Virgin Mary are bleeding because of the many sins, sacrileges, and blasphemies piercing them as penetrating and prickly thorns. Pray the Rosary and offer it in reparation to Jesus and Mary for the crimes and sins of the whole world. The world is about to face great calamities and dangers, and if reparations, sacrifices and prayers are not offered, it may fall into the large abyss which it has reached. I, the Archangel St. Gabriel, invite you to honor the Most Blessed Virgin Mary, Mother of God, by praying the Rosary, asking Her powerful intercession and protection, since only She can come to your aid in the presence of God Our Lord. Pray, pray, pray!

The message of September 19, 1995, offers another invitation to the young people of the world to turn towards Christian holiness and purity, and away from the many pleasures and temptations that the world offers them today:

Dear young people, I desire to guide you to complete sanctity with God, but first you need to pray constantly and take the path of conversion, sacrifice and penance. I need your help. Help me. Beloved youth, change your lives. Renounce the pleasures of this world. Be pure. Convert yourselves. Satan wants to conquer many young people through persuasion and temptations, but you can overcome him by reciting the Rosary. Convert yourselves now! Do not leave your conversion for tomorrow. I bless everyone who is present here and place you inside my Immaculate Heart. Get together more often to pray. Pray more. Read the Bible, the word of My Son Jesus.

This brief message of November 10, 1995 reiterates the infinite love of the Heavenly Father, and the call to thank him for the inestimable gift of life:

God is your Father and your Creator. Thank Him for the great gift of your lives granted by Him. Life is a very special gift, granted by God to every creature. The Father is loving to all of His children, but only few of them are loving towards the Celestial Father. Love God with all your heart and offer Him all your troubles.

Several Itapiranga messages, including this November 11, 1995 message to priests and bishops, discuss the urgent need to pray for our bishops, priests, and religious. This communication further identifies that many of today's clergy are in need of grave prayer in order to remain faithful to their vocation:

My little ones, do not be unbelieving, but be steadfast in your prayers. Jesus is your peace. Love Jesus and comfort His Heart, which is wounded with love for you. Do not get discouraged my little ones. Take courage. Proceed to the Father's home confidently. Pray for the priests, for the bishops and for the souls who are consecrated to God. Pray, pray for the Holy Church. The Church needs numerous prayers and sacrifices. Many favorite sons are in great need of your prayers to remain firm to the vocation they have been called. They count on your prayers and sacrifice. Pray little ones, pray, pray. The world needs a great deal of prayers and sacrifices. Satan works intensely in this world, trying to destroy every child of the Lord. Satan wants to destroy your lives, my children; thus come to my arms, so that I can protect you from his attacks and traps. I am your Celestial Mother and I am here to defend you from all evil. Free yourselves from sin and confess; then you will be able to take the path that leads to salvation, which is Jesus.

The following weighty message revealed in late Fall of 1995 warns of a soon approaching purification for humanity, and the global need for true repentance, particularly, for those involved in the grave sin of Abortion:

> *The cup of Divine Justine is full and overflowing. Soon, great events will destabilize all humanity, renewing all 'mankind. The great purification will soon take place. Cleanse yourselves now from your sins; free yourselves through holy confession, so that you can endure the day of the coming of the Lord. To the mothers who do not want the children in their wombs to be born and desire to kill them (I say): Repent, repent! For God's anger will fall upon those mothers and fathers who are murderers. Pray to the end of abortion. Pray to the end of violence. Pray much for those who do not believe in God. Do penances for the poor sinners.*
>
> *My little children, wipe away the tears from your Mother's face, caused by the innumerable sins committed in the world. Many people offend the Lord. Many blaspheme against His Holy name. Make reparation for these terrible sins. Help me, little children. Your celestial Mother awaits for your help. Pray for Brazil. Again, I say to you: if the Brazilian people do not heed my requests, a great punishment will come upon your nation. Pray for it. Jesus loves your nation so much. Pray for it. He has a special grace to accomplish here in Brazil.*

On Christmas Day, 1995, St. Michael delivers a tender and encouraging message regarding the protection Our Lady grants to all families open to her maternal care. The Archangel furthermore exhorts humanity to obey the messages of

Itapiranga, while at the same time re-affirming the infinite love of Jesus, "King of Families":

> *Our Lady has her mantle placed upon your families. Jesus and Mary wish to live in your hearts and in your families. They desire to teach you to take the path of sanctity in the families. Thus, your family has been chosen to be an example to the others. This way, they wish to show other families how much they love them. Jesus and Mary wish that all families open their doors to receive them. The Virgin Mary teaches, exhorts and invites you. She wants to guide you but you still do not listen to Her words. It is very important that you be obedient.*

> *Our Lord, the King of all families, wishes to be with you. Know that He loves you and it was Him who has sent me. Do you understand what I tell you? It is God who has sent me to you. He is the Almighty, Creator of Heaven and Earth, the God of Abraham, the God of Isaac, and the God of Jacob, according to the Scriptures. He is everything, the Lord of the universe. You have not yet understood it? It is necessary that you open your hearts more. Say to the Lord always:* **Lord, open my heart so that I will be able to understand your word as Our Lady does. Amen!**

In summary, the 1995 second year of Itapiranga messages brought forth a relative abundance of inspired words which contained delicate balance of peace and urgency, of admonition and love, which overall does not intend to frighten, but to elicit response. The global reality conveyed in these celestial communications should rightly bring forth a generous and committed response in living these messages, as the conversion and salvation of countless souls throughout the world depend on it.

The final pithy message of 1995 (December 30ᵗʰ) illustrates God's need for co-redeeming cooperation on the part of humanity for the ultimate success of Heaven's desires at Itapiranga, and against Satan's intentions to prevent it:

Jesus to Edson:

Fight my son, so that Satan does end up destroying my plans.

The Itapiranga messages of the following year, 1996, will both return to and further cultivate the themes revealed in 1995, but also will introduce some new and powerful themes. For the sake of staying true to the intent of this small work, that is, to provide you with a *brief* introduction to the basic message of Itapiranga, we will not go through each 1996 message here, but a complete presentation of all of the messages selected by Edson from the year 1996 can be found in Chapter 6.

In the next chapter, we will turn to the 1997 Itapiranga messages and the gradual unveiling of the most quintessential theme of these heavenly interventions from the Amazonas: **the union of the Three Hearts and its critical efficacy for today's Church and world**.

CHAPTER III

THE THREE HEARTS

The year 1997 would bring supernatural announcements that would provide greater development of heavenly calls already given, but also new declarations. This was inclusive of messages which would contribute to the gradual revelation of the unique and principal charism of the entire Itapiranga phenomenon: a *united devotion to the "Three Hearts."*

While it is true that some messages pertaining to the Three Hearts were presented in seed form from as early as May, 1994 (for example, the vision granted to Edson of the Three Hearts of the Holy Family), the messages of 1997 will further develop this essential theme of the unity and efficacy of the Hearts of Jesus, Mary, and Joseph. They will serve as a theological and thematic segue to the extraordinary novena of Messages from March 1-9, 1998, which will emphatically and universally call for devotion and consecration to the newly introduced "Third Heart"—the "Most Chaste Heart of St. Joseph."

Once again, some of the key messages delivered during 1997 will be provided here, while all the Itapiranga messages revealed during this year and selected by the visionary, Edson Glauber, are located in Chapter 6.

The Queen of the Rosary and of Peace wastes no time in 1997 in renewing the call for praying for the sanctification of the family. In this January 1, 1997 communication, Our Lady also underscores the vital role of women in domestic holiness:

> *Dear children,*
>
> *I have a very special plan for the families. If all families live deeply my holy messages, soon many will be sanctified by Divine Grace. All families belong to the Heavenly Family, but will only remain faithful to it if they live in permanent union with God. God cherishes families and He blesses them through the heart of His Son Jesus, and the Immaculate Heart of His Heavenly Mother.*
>
> *My daughters, mothers and wives, pray that Satan may not take possession of your homes, your husbands and children. You are responsible for them. Mothers and wives, God has a very special affection for you. Women's dignity is in being mothers. If mothers knew how precious the gift of motherhood is, they would never abort their children. Penance, penance, penance. Renounce sin with all your heart. Pray and you will be freed from sin.*

On the next day, January 2nd, the Mother of Jesus reiterates the absolute imperative of praying the Rosary each day, and doing so "within the heart" of the Catholic Church:

> *You still don't understand the importance of praying the Rosary. If you knew the value of praying the Rosary, you would pray it on a daily basis without ever failing. Many of my children are lazy to pray. Bear in mind, children, that laziness does not come from God. If you have not been able to renounce laziness, you should start now, so that God does not renounce you on the final days of your life,*

because laziness is a sin and sin drives you away from my Son Jesus Christ. Do not be lazy to pray, because if you keep praying, you will be leading the way toward salvation. Salvation is achieved only through prayer, man's effort and good will to do all that God asks for, through his holy Word and holy Church which, once again I tell you, is the Catholic Church.

On the same day, Jesus Himself warns against the profanation of Church tabernacles and sanctuaries through immodest dress:

Oh beloved children, do not ever allow my tabernacles to be ever profaned and ravaged, because of the great violations against my Church perpetrated by many of my children, who don't know how to value and respect my holy temple. It is the immodesty of many of my daughters, by wearing the most immoderate outfits when coming to my sanctuary, and thus hurting my Sacred Heart and tormenting me even more, increasing the pain of my Holy Wounds. Oh my beloved children, care for the honor and glory of your God. Do not remain silent before such great desecration inside my Sanctuary. Warn my daughters about this great dishonor to their God. I am the thrice Holy and I abhor any stain of sin. I desire to see all of you shining in sanctity. I desire to enrich you with my Divine Grace, beloved children. You are my worthy representatives. You are my anointed ones. You are loved by Me and my heavenly Mother in a special way. Blessed is the priest who has my Mother as his intercessor, and foremost, as his mother. I will not leave him unattended in his prayers, and in his most difficult times.

This January 25, 1997 message from Our Lady stresses that only a priest can forgive sins through the sacrament of Confession (and this in a region where Protestant evangelism is leading great numbers of Brazilians to leave the Catholic Church):

> *Son, only a priest has the right and the grace given by God to forgive sins. Without confession there is no salvation. Children, know how to long for each creature God has created. Animals are to be treated with love and affection, because they are God's creatures. But they should not be treated as if they were humans.*

February 3rd marks a vision of the Crucified Jesus and a call to faithfulness to the unconditionally sacrificial love of Jesus for humanity, which is ultimately proven on the Cross:

> *Faithfulness: the one who is faithful to my words I will never forget him on his trials nor on the last moment of his life.*

> *I am the true Life. Give your lives to me so that you may be living people, not dead ones. Do you know what was my biggest proof of love?*

Edson: At this point, I saw Jesus on the cross, on the moment of His crucifixion, on Mount Calvary, surrounded by a multitude of people mocking Him. Jesus prayed saying.

> *Father, forgive them because they don't know what they are doing. I love them, but they hate me. I forgive them, but they condemn me. I am here with opened arms to receive them all, but they refuse to come to me. I want all of you with me, by my side. I love you so!*

On the same day and soon after the vision of Jesus on the Cross, Edson saw another vision which conveys the present lack of faithfulness and sacrificial love in many marriages today. It begins with a vision of a hand with a wedding ring on one finger which then dramatically breaks:

Edson: During the prayer, I saw a hand with a ring on one of the fingers. After a few moments this ring broke up, becoming unusable. I asked Our Lady the meaning of this vision, to what She answered:

> *These are marriages destroyed by the unfaithfulness of husbands and wives, who do not fulfill the vows done before God's Altar, before my Son Jesus, when they got married. Warn all couples about this serious fault: of not being faithful to this vow that they have made before my Son Jesus, at the time of their wedding.*

On February 11, 1997, the anniversary of the Marian apparitions at Lourdes, Our Lady relays a truly sobering message. She prophesies a time of "great darkness for the Church" and predicts the martyrdom of many, including priests:

> *Dear children, I come to tell you that the times of great darkness for the Church are approaching. How painful, dear children, it is to tell you this: evil men will persecute my poor and dear favorite children until they bleed. Many will be martyred for their love of God and of the Holy Church. I wish to tell all my sons who are priests that I am with them, at their side, to receive their sacrifice and immolation. I present all of them before God every day so that my Lord will strengthen them in faith and love.*

Once again, the Mother of the Holy Family stresses the critical importance of "mothers and wives" in the proper spiritual formation of the "domestic church." In this February 26th message, she calls children *"the most precious jewels God has given you"* and speaks of the contaminating influence of the television as an *"evil idol"*:

> *My dear daughters, mothers and wives, take care of your children with a loving heart. Your children are the most precious jewels that God has granted you. Bless them always, and never let the wickedness of this world approach them. How can this take place? By allowing your children to learn the worst things that are broadcast today on TV. The television is an evil idol that man has created to serve the Enemy, instead of God. If they knew how to use the means of communication to build the kingdom of God, that would be great. But today, men just use it for the progress of the evil in the world. Pray for all those that teach horrible and wrong things to all children, for they will not escape the Divine Justice, because they are destroying my Son Jesus' little angels in this world.*

March 1st brings a communication from the Mother of the Church which again reiterates that the *"truth is only found in the Catholic Church."* She likewise summons the Christian faithful to pray to the Holy Spirit for enlightenment as to where to find the authentic truth:

> *Dear children, I beg you: flee from sin. Do not search for God in places where His word is not correctly lived. Truth is only found in the Catholic Church. Many errors are spread throughout the world because people no longer pray to Holy Spirit asking for enlightenment. Pray to the Holy Spirit and He will show you the Truth. Do not ask me so many questions, but rather listen to Me. The current*

times are not very good. Urgent conversion of all peoples
is necessary. I invite all of you: come back to God, truly.

In the message of March 3, 1997, Our Lady reveals a prayer of Consecration to the Holy Family for family protection again the evils of the world, and to bring forth a full love and imitation of the Family of Nazareth:

Families whose foundation is upon the world will never
remain standing. Families whose foundation is based
on God and His love will remain standing and intact,
and my Enemy will not approach them. Pray, always
my children:

Oh Holy Family of Nazareth, Jesus, Mary and Joseph,
on this moment we truly consecrate ourselves to You, with
all our hearts. Protect and defend us against the evils of
this world so that our homes may always be steady on
God's infinite love. Jesus, Mary, and Joseph, we love you
with all our hearts. We want to be all yours. Help us to do
the will of the Lord, truly. Guide us always to heavenly
Glory, now and forever more. Amen!

Another instruction on the imperative for modesty and purity comes from the Virgin Most Pure. In this March 4, 1997 message, she gives very specific guidelines on what type of dress is appropriate and what is inappropriate for attendance and participation at Holy Mass:

My peace I give to all of you!

I say it again: I want you to be respectful when you pray
in this place, or when you gather together with the people

to pray. Be well-dressed, also receive those who are well-dressed, that is, men are to wear long pants and shirts with sleeves; women shall be wearing a dress or a skirt. Dresses and blouses are to be with sleeves. The longer the better. Women's garments should be loose to the body. When they wear clothes tight to the body, they look like a snake, of a poisonous kind.

Women are not advised to wear pants and shorts, but when they do wear them, they should be loose to the body and, the shorts are to be below the knees; and men´s are to be to the knees. These kinds of clothes are fitting when you are at ease at home, or traveling, or at the beach, whereas when at Church in prayer or in prayer groups, you should all dress modestly and with no ostentation: as simple as possible. Thank you for answering us. We bless you: in the name of the Father, the Son, and of the Holy Spirit. Amen!

In a message to Edson's mother, Maria, Our Lady emphatically and repeatedly calls for spreading the Itapiranga message "to the whole world" (March 16, 1997):

May my peace be with all of you! My daughter Maria do Carmo, propagate, propagate, propagate this message to the whole world: whoever offends and humiliates someone here on earth, it is Me and My Son Jesus Christ that he offends and humiliates. Thank you for answering Me. I bless you in the name of the Father, of the Son, and of the Holy Spirit. Amen! Amen!

The Solemnity of the Annunciation (March 25th) provides the occasion for a global Gospel call from the Queen of Peace to "come back" to faith in Jesus Christ and His Church, as her purpose in coming is precisely to encourage humanity to achieve its salvation:

> *May my peace be with all of you! Tell all sinners: come back, come back, come back as soon as possible. I tell you over and over again: convert, flee from vices, despise sin. Sin, my little children, is the enemy of my Son Jesus. That is why My Son and I cry so much, tears of blood. Don't be afraid to come back to Jesus, who alone is your Savior and the Savior of the whole world.*
>
> *Humanity has not yet entrusted itself to God. So many years have gone by and many people still do not mind about the Father, the Son, and the Holy Spirit. Why so much disobedience, little children of mine?*
>
> *I am the **Queen of Peace** and your heavenly mother. I am very much concerned about all those who don't care about my presence here on the Earth. I come to you for a special reason: to warn you, for your salvation.*
>
> *I tell you again, come back to my Son Jesus because He is everything in your life. Thank you for answering Me. I bless you in the name of the Father, of the Son, and of the Holy Spirit. Amen. Amen.*

April 3rd brings a call for forgiveness, which includes a general reference for forgiveness within our families and the specific directive for parents to *"ask forgiveness from your children."* This Marian message is then followed by a communication from Jesus to Maria, which reveals to her a prayer that is to be said before the Blessed Sacrament in reparation for the infinite offenses which so saddens the Sacred Heart of our Savior:

Queen of Peace: My peace to all of you, children of mine! Ask for daily forgiveness for the faults you have committed, especially this year. This is not only the year of the family, but it is also the year to forgive and to ask for forgiveness.

Father and mother, ask your children´s forgiveness for the faults you have committed. Children ask your parent´s forgiveness for the faults you have committed.

Each person must ask his brethren for forgiveness of the wrongs committed. You must ask for forgiveness and always forgive when they commit transgressions.

Thank you for answering me. I bless you in the name of the Father, of the Son, and of the Holy Spirit. Amen. Amen, Jesus!

Our Lord, Jesus: I also bless you in the name of the Father, of the Son, and of the Holy Spirit. Amen. Amen!

Edson: Jesus, very sad and sorrowful, told my mother:

Daughter, when I see so many perversities in the world, My Heart breaks in many pieces and It hurts very much. Cherish me before the Most Blessed Sacrament of the altar. Say this:

Heavenly Father, I love You. Lay here on my shoulder. I want to cherish you and to ask for forgiveness for all those who do not know how to cherish you and make an apology to You. Forgive me, Lord. Amen

While Edson was in the State of San Paolo (April 14, 1997), St. Michael the Archangel appeared and made known to Edson a prayer of Consecration to the Immaculate Virgin, which should be prayed with love and affection for our common Mother:

Peace from the Lord and Our Most Holy Virgin to all of you!

I am St. Michael the Archangel and I come to you, at the request of Jesus and the Most Holy Mary. Jesus wishes that all of you receive His Most Holy Mother with much love and affection, and that you recite the prayer I am going to teach you now:

"Oh Mary, Virgin Most Holy and Immaculate, bless us and protect us against all evil. Right now we truly entrust ourselves to You, heart, soul and body. Oh Mother of God, be our salvation now and on the last moment of our life. Lead us to Jesus and pray for us to Our Lord that He may give us His Peace and Love. Amen!"

Pray, pray, pray. This is a request from the Virgin Mother. I bless you all on behalf of the Lord and of the Virgin Mary, in the name of the Father, of the Son, and of the Holy Spirit. Amen. Amen! See you soon!

The Solemnity of the Sacred Heart of Jesus, June 6, 1997, would bring a monumental message, with a historic request that came directly from our divine Redeemer. On this day, Jesus requests a feast day to be instituted in the Church in honor of "the Most Chaste Heart of St. Joseph." Our Lord further directs that this new feast is to be celebrated on the first Wednesday which follows the movable liturgical celebrations of the Sacred Heart of Jesus (Friday) and the Immaculate Heart of Mary (on the Saturday which immediately follows the solemnity of the Sacred Heart):

Children of mine, I love you so. Men have not yet understood the infinite value of My love for them. If you knew how much love I have for you, you would cry for joy. I am your Eternal Salvation, the Source of Mercy and Grace.

My children, always try to feel Me close to you through prayer, prayed from the heart. I seek in the whole world for a soul that wishes to faithfully serve Me, but I find only a few. My children, do not waste so many graces. I come from heaven to place you all into My Sacred Heart. If you want to receive graces, you must have unlimited trust in my Sacred Heart. Ask anything with faith, you will receive it. Love, love, love. The more you love, the more you will receive from Me, whatever you ask for.

I desire that the first Wednesday, after the Feast of my Sacred Heart and the Immaculate Heart of Mary, be dedicated to the Feast of the Most Chaste Heart of St. Joseph.

Edson: I understood that it was the Wednesday following these two Feasts of the Sacred of Heart of Jesus and the Immaculate Heart of Mary. On that year, the feast of the Sacred Heart of Jesus was on June 6th; the feast of the Immaculate Heart on June 7th; and the feast of the Most Chaste Heart of St. Joseph was on Wednesday, June 11th. It was the first time Jesus revealed to me the day of the feast of the Most Chaste Heart of St. Joseph. We celebrated this feast at the Church of the Sacred Family in Ghiaie di Bonate, as I was in Italy with Father Vincenzo Savoldi.

Our Lady calls the youth in this June 8th message to see the Immaculate Heart as their special refuge and protection, and to consecrate themselves to the Immaculate Heart entirely, body and soul, on a daily basis. She also encourages the youth to open their hearts fully to the love of Jesus:

> *My little ones, you are to be a living light shining God's Love in this world. Your lives are to be holy and pure. God has plans of mercy for all of you.*

> *Dear youth, my Immaculate Heart is your refuge for protection. Consecrate everyday your thoughts, your bodies, and your souls to God, so that He may protect you against all evil. Live a life of faith. Always have confidence in God and also in My Immaculate Heart. Dear youth, open your hearts to Jesus. May your hearts burn with love for Jesus, so that He may mold your hearts, transforming them totally.*

More pivotal messages regarding devotion to St. Joseph's Most Chaste Heart come from Our Lady, Jesus, and then St. Joseph himself, in apparitions which take place on the requested "Feast Day of the Most Chaste Heart of St. Joseph," which in 1997 fell on Wednesday, June 11, 1997. Our Lady exhorts that *"the whole world should have a great love to the Most Chaste Heart of St. Joseph."* The Blessed Mother also makes reference to a series of apparitions of the Holy Family that took place Ghiaie di Bonate in northern Italy during the 1940s—apparitions in which devotion to St. Joseph was also accentuated:

> *Dear children, when I appeared in Ghiaie di Bonate with Jesus and St. Joseph I wanted to show you that later on the whole world should have a great love to the Most Chaste Heart of St. Joseph and to the Holy Family, because Satan would attack the families very profoundly in this end of*

times, destroying them. But I come again, bringing the graces of God Our Lord, to grant them to all the families most in need of Divine protection.

Jesus conveyed the following message:

Love, love, love the Most Chaste Heart of My Virginal Father Joseph. Give yourself totally to this Pure, Most Chaste and Virginal Heart, because My Sacred Heart has shaped It to be My vessel of graces to sinful humanity, as the Immaculate Heart of My Mother, the Most Holy Mary.

He who has a deep devotion to the Most Chaste Heart of St. Joseph will not be eternally lost. This is the great promise, which I do here in this Holy place.

Edson: On this day, St. Joseph sent me his message:

The Divine Savior and My Spouse the Most Blessed Mary allow me to grant you all graces. I will pray intensely to Jesus and Mary for you.

Then, the Three said together:

We, the Holy Family, bless you: in the name of the Father, of the Son, and of the Holy Spirit. Amen. Farewell!

❧ ⟨⟩ ☙

The Marian communication of June 13, 1997 conveys a multiform prayer call for priests, the souls in Purgatory, the youth, and a strong admonition to mothers and fathers who abort their children, since *"abortion is a demonic work:"*

Edson: What do You have to say to the priests?

May the priests be pure and holy.

The priests have received the divine mission to bring Jesus to all men through the Holy Sacraments. Jesus is present, sharply/deeply, in the Holy Sacraments, granting them His love and graces in the Holy Eucharist, His forgiveness in the Holy Sacrament of Confession, because He earnestly desires your eternal salvation.

I invite you tonight to pray much for the most needy souls in purgatory. Pray, pray, pray.

Live the Word of God deeply. Spread the devotion to the Sacred Hearts to your brothers and sisters.

Pray for those children who are in danger of being aborted from their mothers' womb. Fathers and mothers who abort their children are no longer human persons, but true images of Satan because abortion is a demonic work in the world.

May all young people seek to live a life of intimate union with Jesus, so that Jesus may give them the strength and grace necessary to overcome the snares of Satan. Tonight your Heavenly Mother blesses you with the blessing of peace: in the name of the Father, the Son and of the Holy Spirit. Amen. See you then!

And again, on July 2nd, Our Lady calls us to "flee from sin:"

You still are not able to be profoundly united with God because of your weakness of falling into various sins. Flee from all sin, so that the Grace of my Lord may be expanded in your lives.

Children, pray for all those who commit adultery. They do not know how dangerous this sin is. If people do not sincerely renounce this sin, asking the Lord for forgiveness, they will be in danger of being lost forever. Do not allow sin to destroy your souls. Tonight, meditate deeply on this message of mine: you still have many weaknesses that make it impossible for you to understand my Motherly love and God's love, because you are attached to worldly things. Pray, pray, pray and you will be free from all slavery of sin and, thus, God's love will transform you wholly.

How truly important is the role of daughters, mothers, and wives, as the Queen of Families expressly beseeches them to consecrate themselves each day to Her Immaculate Heart, and likewise to avoid serious sins which so grieve the Sacred Heart of her Son (July 6, 1997):

Dear children, tonight I especially bless all mothers and My Son Jesus blesses in a special way all my other children.

Dearest daughters, mothers and wives, I turn once again to all of you: you must live a profound life of prayer and consecrate yourself every day to my Immaculate Heart, as well as your families, so that you may be protected by my Lord, Who has entrusted me to you to be your protector and the Queen of your families.

Daughters, fear nothing before me, even though your homes are being violently attacked by my Enemy. I tell you: I am here to protect you all. I ask you for an unlimited trust in my Motherly protection.

I love you, I love you, I love you, my dear children. If you want to know deeply my Motherly love and the love of My Son Jesus, you must surrender yourself to us without reservation, because we truly surrender ourselves to you with all our love. Pray, pray and you may understand

*the value of our presence among you. Be faithful to my
Son Jesus. Do not let His Sacred Heart grieve seeing
you falling into serious sin. This is my request and my
message tonight.*

The Rosary is the prayer "that will change the most
difficult situations that are affecting the whole world." Our
Lady directly identifies the Rosary as the "most effective
weapon God gives" in overcoming any difficulty or obstacle
(July 8, 1997):

*Dear children, pray, pray, pray. Tell everyone to pray the
Holy Rosary always, for it is with this prayer that we
will change the most difficult situations that are affecting
the whole world today. Know how to give to prayer
a great value. It is the most effective weapon that God
gives you in any difficult situation and obstacle that arises
in your lives.*

*Dear children, if you live my messages, you will help me
to accomplish the triumph of my Immaculate Heart in the
world more and more, and especially in the hearts of your
brethren, for all will know the love of my son Jesus, they
will feel His peace and then be converted.*

"Come to me, for the time of Mercy is running out," Jesus reveals
in this July 10th transmittance:

*Little children, wake up, wake up. As I have already
told you: woe to those who mocked and outraged my Holy
Mother, her apparitions and her holy messages. They will
have to settle an account with me one day. And I say to
you that, on that day when they will settle an account*

with me, they shall not find me as a Merciful God, but a God of justice, for my justice is also great. If you want my mercy and my love, do not miss the opportunity, my little children. I easily forgive you if you sincerely ask for forgiveness and if you repent of your acts, but hurry up; come to me, for the time of Mercy is running out. I tell you that if it had not been for my Holy Mother and her apparitions in the world asking for My Mercy and Love, my Divine Justice would have already fallen upon you a long time ago. But for the prayers of my Mother, once again Mercy overcame justice.

August 5th is the feast of "Our Lady of the Snows," which celebrates the fourth century Marian visions in Rome which led to the construction of the most ancient basilica dedicated to the Mother of God, *Santa Maria Maggiore* (St. Mary Major). A few days earlier, on August 2nd, Our Lady makes reference to the most beautiful "gift" for her for this feast, which is to see her earthly children united through love:

If you want to give me a gift on August 5th, the most beautiful gift would be to see you united as true brothers and sisters, living peace and love among you. Love, love, love, otherwise you will only bring unhappiness to yourselves.

May you dedicate yourselves this week to help those who have been cause of disagreement and loneliness to others and to their families.

May you be united to the person who has difficulty to communicate and to love. To all a very affectionate Mother's blessing. I bless you and invite you to be a light

*in this world, and not an obstacle in the conversion of
your brethren.*

The recurrent Itapiranga summons for the holiness of priests
signifies its prominent importance for the Church today
(September 6, 1997):

*May the priests be holy, truly holy, because God is thrice
Holy, and He desires that His ministers live sanctity and
spread it wherever they go. A priest who does not pray and
live the daily prayer united to God does not fulfill His Will.*

*Priests ought to live the prayer intensely, because it is in
prayer that Lord God grants them the graces and the light
necessary to faithfully lead His flock.*

*I beg all priests to listen to my call. Only in this way they
will be able to solve the most difficult problems and will
have the necessary strength to carry out the mission that
Jesus assigned to them. It is through prayer united to God
that they may even be able to perform wonderful deeds
and obtain great miracles from the Heart of Jesus.*

"Everything can be changed by my Son, Jesus" is Our Lady's
wisdom concerning the upcoming "terrible" suffering for
humanity. At the same time, we must cease sinning on a global
scale and begin obeying the commands of God (message to
Maria, October 6, 1997):

The peace of My Son Jesus and My Peace to all of you!

*I am your Heavenly Mother and I come to warn you
once more. I am very worried about what is going to*

happen to the world if you do not pray with faith and love in your heart.

Everything can be changed by My Son Jesus, if you obey my appeals. Change is for the good of all people of the whole world. If they do not obey, humanity's suffering will be terrible. That is why I ask you to obey. Thank you for answering me!

I bless you all: in the name of the Father, the Son and the Holy Spirit. Amen. See you soon!

On October 12, 1997, Our Lady reminds us of the vital importance of confession:

Dear children, today I wish to talk to you about the importance of confession. If you do not confess regularly you will be in danger of being lost eternally. Many do not approach the Sacrament of Confession to sincerely ask for forgiveness of their sins and this worries me, because these children of mine are far from the Heart of My Son Jesus and from My Immaculate Heart.

Dear children, many are those who confess only by habit, but remain the same afterwards. Convert deeply and repent from your sins.

I am united here, vividly present, and I look at each of you with Motherly tenderness. I am your Mother and I want to help you in your needs and afflictions.

On October 13, 1997, the eightieth anniversary of the great "Solar Miracle" at Fatima, Our Lady prophetically warns us that, "punishments will come in greater proportions if you do not convert":

> *I ask all my priest sons to be, first of all, model and example, for all my other children in the faith.*
>
> *Priests, listen to me: I am your Queen and the Mother of God and I come to help you to faithfully fulfill the mission that My Son Jesus entrusted to you.*
>
> *My children, today you are celebrating My last apparition at Fatima, to My three little shepherds. So many years ago I spoke at Fatima, giving My message, but men remain deaf. They do not want to obey what the Lord has recommended through Me. I tell you, that now as never before, listening to my Motherly appeals has become more imperative, because difficult moments are approaching you, my children. Punishments will come in greater proportions if you do not convert. Humanity is destroying itself more and more with the leprosy of sin.*
>
> *Children, wake up. Live my messages. I want to save you from these tribulations. I come not to frighten you, but to warn them.*

We conclude our survey of key Itapiranga messages of 1997 with this extremely challenging message regarding the priesthood. On October 20, 1997, Edson received an intense communication from Jesus which Our Lord described as "my holy message that is destined for all the priests":

Edson: Tonight, Jesus directed me to a passage from the Holy Scriptures: Isaiah 56: 9-12; 57: 4.

Come, my dear son, write my holy message that is destined to all the priests. Do not waste time and pay attention to all that I will say about the reading that has been given to you. Today My priests are as asleep. A thick darkness surrounds many of My favorite children. Some of them have let themselves be involved in darkness, because they did not have a life of intimate union with Me, even though being priests of My Church. Look at My Church! From heaven I see My Church so desolate, living moments of great confusion and even of great rebellion. There are many who no longer have faith. They are with their hearts as cold as ice. There is no one who is willing to listen to me, through My Church and especially through the voice of My representative in the world, the pope ... Children priests, listen to the voice of your God. Remain faithful to the pope. You must be to the sheep entrusted to you a sign of holy example and obedience. Woe to the priests who did not know how to care for the flock entrusted to them. Woe to the bad priest, the one who cared more about his own interests and the things of the world than about My interests and the things of heaven. To these priests My Divine Justice is weighing heavily, if they do not sincerely repent of their faults.

Edson: But Lord, if they repent, will they be forgiven?

Yes, if they repent, they will receive My forgiveness. But it is necessary that all listen to this My appeal to them. Many have become deaf, they have closed their hearts because they no longer want to free themselves from worldly things and their wrong doings, and thus stifle My voice, which calls them to return and repent. They stifle My voice that speaks to them inside their hearts. Favorite children, have you not realized that you are united with Me through the priesthood? Then why do you make Me suffer so much with your betrayals, like

Judas who betrayed Me, often committing terrible sins? To My consolation, I still have a number of priests who remain faithful to My precepts and teachings, and are obedient to My voice and to the voice of my beloved Pope. Through this message I call all priests to return to Me in faithfulness, renewing their promise to remain committed to their apostolic mission. To all my favorite children My Holy Blessing, that they may ask, through the intercession of the Immaculate Heart of my Holy Mother and of the Most Chaste Heart of my Virginal Father St. Joseph, the grace of being true examples of holiness for all the faithful. I bless my children priests of the world over: in the name of the Father, the Son and the Holy Spirit. Amen!

Jesus taught two prayers for the priests:

Lord, sanctify all priests by the merits of Your Holy Passion, so that they may be your true image, pure and holy in the world. Amen!

Lord, by the bitterness you felt for Judas' treacherous kiss, bring back to the sanctifying grace all the priests who were unfaithful to their vocation and who remain obstinate in the sins of the world. This we ask through the intercession of the Immaculate Heart of Mary and of the Most Chaste Heart of St. Joseph. Amen!

A good mother does not hide the truth from her children. During 1997, the Queen of the Rosary and of Peace relays serious revelations to the human family for the sake of much needed conversion, as well as crucial mitigation for the global rejection of God, His law, and His love. The Mother seeks to motivate our hearts to a new generosity of prayer and penance in her efforts to renew the foundational Fatima message in the twenty-first century for one unified goal: world peace, which is only attainable through the spiritual peace of Jesus Christ in the hearts of humanity.

CHAPTER IV

THE MOST CHASTE HEART OF JOSEPH

T he message of Itapiranga opens a new and resplendent chapter in the history of authentic private revelation concerning the truth about the Virginal Father of Jesus, the pure Spouse of Mary, and the spiritual Father of all humanity. This epic epiphany concerning the good and just St. Joseph is wondrously embodied in the inspired title and role of "*the Most Chaste Heart of Joseph.*"

What do we mean when we refer to the "heart" of someone? Typically, we mean something more than simply the biological organ which pumps blood to the body.

Scripturally, the word "heart" indicates far more than just a body part. "Heart" in the Bible signifies the core of the person, his or her "inner self," and in some cases represents the entirety of the person in question. The term *heart* represents the fullness of the human being, the seat of the faculties of the soul, which, along with being the source of his desires and emotions, also include the higher faculties of the human soul, that is, the human person's capacity to think, as exercised through the intellect, and his or her ability to love, as manifest through the will.

When we discuss devotion to the "heart" of someone, we mean, therefore, beyond his physical dimension, the source of who he or she is in their very being, in an expression—all that a person is and all that a person does. It is sometimes quipped that in the Western world, man thinks of himself as a "mind," but in Eastern cultures, a human being is more typically described as a "heart."

In short, *heart* signifies *person*.

In the case of the traditional Catholic devotion to the Sacred Heart of Jesus, we adore the physical heart of Jesus, as the ultimate "relic of relics" worthy of our adoration, in as much as it is a material manifestation of his Incarnate love for us as the Second Person of the Trinity made man. But we also worship the "spiritual" aspect of Jesus' Heart, that is, his human faculties of reason and will, memory and emotions which, hypostatically united to his divine Person, merits our authentic acts of adoring love. In terms of the Sacred Heart of Jesus, we also identify the "divine" aspect of His Heart, in that He is truly God the Son made man, and his divinity is an attribute of his Sacred Heart as well. This is why the Sacred Heart of Jesus is alone worthy what we theologically refer to as the worship of "Latria," that is, the type of worship that is appropriate to God alone in virtue of his sole divinity and his absolute lordship and dominion over all creation.

The Catholic Church also joyfully venerates the Immaculate Heart of Mary. St. John Eudes, the great "theologian of the Two Hearts," speaks as well of the three aspects of Mary's Heart and why we should rightly give her Immaculate human Heart our devout Christian honor and love. The physical aspect of Mary's heart is worthy of our veneration, just as a physical bodily relic of any saint deserves our special respect and devotion in light of its physical unity with a sanctified soul. In Our Lady's case, this Heart, as part of her physical body, would never experience material corruption due to her Immaculate Conception, which led to Mary's preservation from Original Sin and all of its effects.

The "spiritual" aspect of Mary's Heart contained her uniquely sanctified intellect and will, memory and emotions, which is why she merits the title of "Immaculate," in virtue of Our Lady's unique prerogative of being entirely "full of grace" (Lk. 1:28). St. John Eudes also identifies the "divine" aspect of Mary's human Heart, not because Mary was herself divine, of course, but rather in light of her participation in the fullness of sanctifying grace, which is precisely to participate in the life and the love of the Trinity. The saints excelled in grace, but Mary alone was "full of grace," and this led to a greater participation by Our Lady in the divine life, as well as a greater divine presence of the Trinity in her Immaculate Heart than any other creature.

For these unique prerogatives of grace and holiness as the Immaculate Virgin Mother of God, the Immaculate Heart of Mary rightly receives the form of devotion theologically referred to as "hyperdulia," which is a veneration which goes beyond, in both nature and degree, the type of devotion given to all other saints and angels (which in contrast is theologically referred to as simply "dulia"). While the appropriate Marian devotion of hyperdulia goes beyond that dulia or veneration due to the angels and saints, it at the same time remains infinitely below the worship of Latria or adoration, which will always be justly and exclusively due to God alone.

The same three elements of physical, spiritual, and even divine aspects present within a human heart, although on its own relatively subordinate level to that of the Hearts of Jesus and Mary, can be said about *the Most Chaste Heart of St. Joseph*. The physical dimension of St. Joseph's Heart is most worthy of our devotion. Joseph's physical heart in as much as it housed a soul which was, according to the best of Josephite theology and tradition, was pre-sanctified in the womb and, according to certain mystical writings, was actually sanctified a moment after his human conception. Popes such as Leo XIII and St. John Paul II indicate that he is the greatest saint after Our Lady. St. Joseph therefore receives in the Church was is referred to as "protodulia," that is, the first place of devotion among all the saints and angels, second only to devotion to the Mother of God. Surely, for the greatest saint after Mary, the body of St. Joseph, which as so intimately united to his pure, chaste, and holy soul, would be deserving of our Christian veneration.

The heart of St. Joseph also contains its "spiritual" dimension, which would include his extraordinarily "just" (biblically, "holy" or "righteous") mind and will, passions, and memory. Certainly, this spiritual aspect of his exceptional heart which so loved, adored, and protected his divine son, and likewise so loved and honored his Immaculate wife, rightfully merits our special respect and veneration. Because St. Joseph's life was the ultimate example of the Christian virtues of purity and chastity, it is most appropriate that these Christian virtues (which, sadly, by way of contrast are so lacking in our present age, particularly among men) should be showcased and underscored in the Heart of the Virginal Father of the Lord and heroic spouse of Our Lady.

Finally, the human Heart of Joseph likewise possesses a truly "divine" aspect, in so far as it is a living temple of the divine presence of God, of the Indwelling of the Most Holy Trinity. It was St. Joseph's heightened and anointed awareness of the Divine Indwelling that fueled and sustained his exceptional virtue, through which St. Joseph participated in the divine life of the Trinity in sanctifying grace to a degree more than any other creature, save for his own Immaculate wife.

Yes, the Most Chaste Heart of Joseph, which encapsulates the entire person, purity, goodness, and love of the Guardian of the Redeemer and husband to the Mediatrix of all graces, rightly calls for—and even demands in the order of Christian justice—our special love, devotion, and imitation.

In light of this theological understanding of the legitimacy of devotion to the Heart of St. Joseph, let us now examine what represents one of the greatest contributions in the history of both Catholic doctrinal development and Catholic private revelation regarding the person of St. Joseph and the appropriate devotion Heaven desires for the most Chaste Heart of St. Joseph, which has been providentially released *now*, at our present critical moment in human history.

The December 25, 1996 vision of the Holy Family, with their three Hearts exposed on the same level, introduced the theme of unity between the Hearts of Jesus, Mary, and Joseph. Once again from a theological perspective, there is unquestionably the primacy of the Sacred Heart of Jesus, as the heart of the God-man, and then followed in hierarchy of value by the Immaculate Heart of Mary. The Most Chaste Heart of St. Joseph would then follow, thirdly, in the order of appropriate devotion. But, this was not the purpose of this early Itapiranga vision—it was rather to emphasize the unity and joint efficacy of the Three Hearts as a source of personal sanctification, family sanctification, and ultimately, global sanctification.

Returning to the 1996 Christmas message concerning the Three Hearts, we notice that both Jesus and Our Lady direct us to appreciate the Heart of Joseph. St. Joseph's Heart appears with the cross of Jesus, and an "M" for Mary which is engraved in the manner of a wound. This wounded M impression symbolizes St. Joseph's coredemptive suffering with Jesus and Mary in the plan of salvation, and is surrounded by twelve white lilies, which represent the purity and sacredness of

St. Joseph's heart, that "has always been pure, chaste, and lived holiness on the highest level." The number "12" further symbolizes St. Joseph's role as "Patriarch of patriarchs" over the twelve tribes of Israel. The visionary, Edson, explains this sublime 1996 Christmas communication:

Edson: It was Christmas day, a Wednesday, at 9:00. I was praying the rosary and as I finished it, I had a very beautiful vision of Our Lady and St. Joseph with the child Jesus. The three were dressed with the most pure golden garments, which tended to assume a clear tone.

Jesus and Our Lady showed their Holy Hearts and pointed with their hands to St. Joseph's Heart, which appeared surrounded by twelve white lilies, and inside of it, the cross of Christ and the "M" for Mary, engraved in the form of a wound.

The twelve white lilies represented purity and sacredness of St. Joseph's Heart, which has always been pure, chaste and has lived holiness at the highest level. It also represents the twelve tribes of Israel, over which St. Joseph reigns as a patriarch. The cross and the letter "M" for Mary engraved in the Heart of St. Joseph meant that St. Joseph loved and deeply imitated Jesus and Mary with His entire heart. They assumed an appearance of wound because St. Joseph shared the sorrows of Jesus and Mary, with His pains, also participating in the mystery of redemption.

From the Hearts of the Child Jesus' and from the Virgin Mary's there were rays of light departing and going towards the Heart of St. Joseph. Those rays represented the one and triune love of Jesus, Mary, and Joseph's hearts, as the Holy Trinity is one and triune in love.

The rays that also are departing from Jesus and Mary's hearts and are reflecting in the heart of St. Joseph shows us that St. Joseph imitated Jesus and Mary in everything and received all the blessings and virtues from their Most Holy Hearts. Jesus and Mary shared everything with him and refused nothing to him, in appreciation for the favors and services dedicated to both. Now, in retribution to so many aids, Jesus and Mary, in an extraordinary manner, request that along with the devotion to their two hearts, to be also glorified and put to devotion the heart of the one they have loved so much in this earth and now, eternally love in heaven: St. Joseph.

The rays that depart from the heart of St. Joseph are made of grace and virtues, as well as all the pure and sacred love that he has received from the hearts of Jesus and Mary, and now he pours over all of those who request his help and the grace from his Most Chaste Heart.

This triune devotion for the Hearts of Jesus, Mary and Joseph, united in one love, glorifies the Holy Trinity, One and Triune, that deeply has poured its grace, blessings and virtues over the Sacred Family of Nazareth.

Jesus Christ, Our Lord, and the Most Holy Virgin asks us this devotion to be practiced, so that the Holy Spirit will perform, as soon as possible, a second Pentecost, pouring His grace, His most pure light and the fire of His love over the whole sinful humanity, which is yet discouraged because of sin to enliven and give humanity a new life: totally sanctifying it as the Holy Family of Nazareth.

The Most Chaste Heart of St. Joseph comes to defend and protect the devotion of the united Hearts of Jesus and Mary, as he has defended them from the persecution of their enemies while on earth.

Now, with the devotion to this Pure and Chaste Heart, the Lord asks the collaboration of St. Joseph, so that He will save the devotion to the Hearts of Jesus and Mary, destroying all the traps, persecutions, and attacks of Satan and his angels against this devotion, protecting and defending it, as well as the Holy Church, with the blessings and grace that comes out of His Heart, during these last times, when there is a great fight between good and evil.

My Glorious St. Joseph: take care of my family today, tomorrow and forever. Amen!

We see, therefore, from Edson's commentary and from the revelation itself, the intense love of the Hearts of Jesus and Mary for the pure and holy Heart of the Head of the Holy Family, both while on earth and now eternally from Heaven, and that They now call the entire world to honor the Most Chaste Heart of Joseph. To do so, if we respond appropriately to this new call for devotion to Joseph's Heart, will lead to a "New Pentecost," a new descent of the Holy Spirit for the Church and for the world, as well as a newfound protection of faith and family from the bold new contemporary attacks of the Adversary upon faith, family, Church, and humanity as a whole.

The request for a new feast day to Joseph's Most Chaste Heart, as previously cited, came from Jesus himself in the message of June 6, 1997:

> *I desire that the first Wednesday, after the Feast of my Sacred Heart and the Immaculate Heart of Mary, be dedicated to the Feast of the Most Chaste Heart of St. Joseph.*

And the call from Jesus to "love, love, love the Most Chaste Heart of My Virginal Father Joseph" came on June 11, 1997:

> *Love, love, love the Most Chaste Heart of My Virginal Father Joseph. Give yourself totally to this Pure, Most Chaste and Virginal Heart because My Sacred Heart shaped it to be My vessel of graces to the sinful humanity, as the Immaculate Heart of My Mother, the Most Holy Mary.*
>
> *He who has a deep devotion to the Most Chaste Heart of St. Joseph will not be eternally lost. This is My great promise, which I do here in this Holy place.*

On the same day, the Immaculate Heart voices her desire that "the whole world should have a great love for the Most Chaste Heart of Joseph," as a particular remedy for family attacks during these "end of times:"

> *Dear children, when I appeared in Ghiaie di Bonate with Jesus and St. Joseph, I wanted to show you that later on the*

whole world should have a great love to the Most Chaste Heart of St. Joseph and to the Holy Family, because Satan would attack the families very profoundly in the end of times, destroying them. But I come again, bringing the graces of God, Our Lord, to grant them to all the families most in need of Divine protection.

St. Joseph himself then said the following:

The Divine Savior and My Spouse, the Most Blessed Mary, allow me to grant you all graces. I will ask much of Jesus and Mary for you.

Finally, the Three Hearts, in one unified voice, declared:

We, the Holy Family, bless you: in the name of the Father, of the Son, and of the Holy Spirit. Amen. See you soon!

All the revelation which comes before in the Itapiranga message regarding St. Joseph reaches its culmination in the March 1 - 9, 1998 novena of messages revealed directly by St. Joseph himself. The beauty in simplicity of these monumental messages in which Heaven voices its emphatic desire for *devotion and consecration to St. Joseph's most chaste Heart today* is in no need of introduction. These heavenly communications, and the numerous "promises" of His Most Chaste Heart which they contain, convey a new level of prophetic revelation which provides an inspired and anointed understanding of the exalted role of St. Joseph with Jesus and Mary in the historic work of Redemption, *both then and now.*

March 1, 1998 – St. Joseph

In this apparition, St. Joseph appeared dressed in a white tunic with a blue robe, accompanied by several angels. St. Joseph held a lily bud and revealed to me his Heart.

> *My dear son, Our Lord God has sent me to tell you about all the graces the faithful will receive from my Most Chaste Heart which Jesus and my blessed spouse wish to be honored. I am St. Joseph and my name means "God will grow," because I grew every day in grace and divine virtues. Through devotion to my Chaste Heart many souls will be saved from the hands of the Devil. God our Lord has allowed for me to reveal to you the promises of my Heart. Just as I am fair and righteous in the sight of God, all who have devotion to my Heart will also be chaste, righteous and holy in His sight. I will fill you with these graces and virtues, making you grow every day on the road of holiness. This is all I will reveal to you on this day. I give my blessing to you my son, and all mankind: in the name of the Father and of the Son and of the Holy Spirit. Amen!*

March 2, 1998 – St. Joseph and the Child Jesus:

St. Joseph appeared with the Child Jesus, with a red mantle and a white tunic. The Boy Jesus had his head inclined on St. Joseph's Heart, playing with the lilies he held in his hands. St. Joseph had brilliant green eyes and a beautiful smile – he appeared to be very young with an indescribable beauty.

The Child Jesus:

> *My son, behold this heart…*

With one of His little hands, the Child Jesus opened the illuminated chest of St. Joseph. In His other hand, Jesus held the Most Chaste Heart of St. Joseph.

Here in this Heart you will find me living, because it is pure and saintly. That all hearts could be like this one, so they could be my home on earth. Imitate this Heart so that you may receive my graces and blessings.

St. Joseph:

My beloved son, today I bless you, I bless your mother and all your family. My beloved son, God, Our Lord, wishes to give all humanity countless graces, through devotion to my heart. My son and Lord Jesus, that I brought up here on earth, with a father's love, desires that all men practice devotion to my Heart, for all those in need of graces from heaven.

He also asks that men help others in need with their good deeds. I promise to all that honor this Most Chaste Heart of mine and who do here on earth good deeds in favor of the most needy, especially of the sick and dying for whom I am a consoler and protector, to receive in their last moment of their lives the grace of a good death. I myself will be to these souls their petitioner to my Son Jesus and, together with my spouse, Most Holy Mary, we will console them in their last hours

here on earth, with our holy presence and they will rest in the peace of our hearts.

Just as you saw my Son Jesus repose His head on my heart, this way myself and my spouse Holy Mary will take these souls to the glory of paradise, in the presence of their Savior, my Son Jesus Christ, so that they may repose, and incline themselves to His Sacred Heart, in the burning furnace of the most pure and loving Heart. I give you my blessing: in the name of the Father and the Son and the Holy Spirit. Amen.

March 3, 1998 – St. Joseph:

St. Joseph came dressed in a white tunic and a white cloak, holding a lily and the Child Jesus, also in white, on his lap.

My beloved son, listen and make it known to all men, what God has permitted me to reveal to you. My beloved son, how sin spreads in a such a strong way! Men let themselves be led by the most insidious wiles of the Devil. The enemy of salvation wants to destroy all men so that, this way, all will be lost. He is envious and hates the entire human race. So many go through trials and temptations, that the enemy of God throws at every moment, this way trying to destroy men's mortal souls that were created by God.

The means that he most utilizes are the sins against holy purity, because purity is one of the virtues most beloved by God, and in this way Satan desires to destroy the image of God present in each creature through this virtue. And it is because of this, that God asks all humanity to have devotion to my Chaste Heart, he wants to give men the grace to overcome the temptations and attacks of the Devil in their day to day lives.

The invocation of my name is enough to make demons flee! I promise to all the faithful that honor my most Chaste Heart with faith and love, the grace to live with holy purity of soul and body and the strength to resist all attacks and temptations by the Devil. I myself will preciously protect you. This grace is not only destined for those who honor this heart of mine, but also for all their family members who are in need of divine help. I give you my blessing: in the name of the Father and of the Son and of the Holy Spirit. Amen.

March 4, 1998 – St. Joseph:

St. Joseph came dressed in a wine-colored cloak with a green tunic. He held a staff in his right hand and showed his Chaste Heart streaming intense rays of light.

My beloved son, today is the first Wednesday of the month. On every first Wednesday of the month, my Chaste Heart pours numerous graces on all who rely on my intercession. On these Wednesdays, men will not receive a shower of simple graces, but very strong torrents of extraordinary graces! I will share them with those who honor me and rely on me, all the blessings, all the virtues, and all the love I received from my Divine Son Jesus and my spouse the Blessed Virgin Mary while still living in this world and all the graces that I continue to receive in the glory of paradise.

My beloved son, what a great honor and grace I received from the Heavenly Father, that made my Heart exult with joy! The Heavenly Father granted me the honor of representing him, in this world, to take care of his Divine and Beloved Son, Jesus Christ. My Heart was also surprised by so much grace, I felt incapable and undeserving of such a great favor and benefit, but I put all in the hands of the Lord and, as his servant, I was ready to do his holy will. Think, my beloved son, what joy I felt in my Heart! The Son of the Most high was now in my care and was known by all men as my legitimate son. To the eyes of the world it was impossible, but for God everything is possible when He so desires it.

Because of this great grace and joy that God granted my Heart and, by such great mystery, I promise to intercede before him for those who come to me, honoring this Heart of mine. I will give them the graces to be able to resolve the most difficult problems and urgent necessities, that to the eyes of man seem impossible, but that, through my intercession to God, will be possible. I grant the graces of my Heart to all sinners so they may convert. My Heart grants its rays of love on the entire Holy Church, particularly on my Son Jesus Christ's Vicar, Pope John Paul II. No one, such as he, has special access to this Heart of mine. That he may trust in my Heart and in my intercession, I am to the Holy Father like a father and protector.

I give my blessing: in the name of the Father and the Son and the Holy Spirit. Amen.

March 5, 1998 – St. Joseph:

The Holy Family appeared: St. Joseph was in a beige cloak and blue grey tunic, in his arms was the Child Jesus wearing a very bright blue tunic. Our Lady was in a white veil and blue grey dress.

My beloved son, my Heart desires to spill many graces this night on all men, because I desire the conversion of all sinners so that they may be saved. That all sinners may not be afraid to approach my Heart, I desire to welcome and protect them. Many are those who are distant from God because of their grave sins. Many of those, my children, are in that state because they let themselves fall to the wiles of the Devil. The enemy of salvation makes them think there is no solution, nor return, because they have despaired and have not trusted in divine mercy. These will be easy targets for the Devil.

But I, my beloved son, tell all sinners, even those who have committed the most terrible sins, to trust in the love and in the forgiveness of God and to trust in me also, in my intercession. All those who trustingly have recourse to me will have the certainty of my help to recover the divine grace and mercy of God. Look, my son, what the Heavenly Father entrusted to me to take care of: his Divine Son Jesus Christ and the Immaculate spouse of the Holy Spirit.

My Heart felt a great peace and joy for having Jesus and Mary at my side in the same house. Our three hearts loved one another. We lived a Trinitarian love, but it was a love united in the act of offering to the Eternal Father. Our hearts melted into the purest love as though becoming one heart living in three persons.

But look, my son, how much my heart grieved and suffered in seeing my Son Jesus so little and already in danger for his life because of Herod that, taken by an evil spirit, ordered the killing of the innocent children. My heart went through great tribulation and suffering because of the great danger my Son Jesus suffered, but our Heavenly Father did not abandon us in that moment, he sent his messenger angel to direct me and what attitude to take in those difficult moments of suffering. Because of this, my son, tell all sinners to not despair in the great dangers of life and in the dangers of losing one's soul.

I promise all who will trust in my most pure chaste Heart, devoutly honoring it, the grace to be consoled by me in their greatest afflictions of the soul and in the danger of judgment, when by misfortune lose divine grace because of their grave sins. To these sinners, who have recourse to me, I promise the graces of my Heart for the purpose of amendment, of repentance and of sincere contrition of their sins. Now, I say to all sinners: Do not be afraid of the Devil and do not despair because of your crimes, but come throw yourselves in my arms and take refuge in my Heart so that you may receive all the graces for your eternal salvation. Now I will give the world my blessing: in the name of the Father and of the Son and of the Holy Spirit. Amen.

March 6, 1998 – St. Joseph:

My beloved son, I would like to speak anew about the graces my Chaste Heart wishes to shower upon all humanity. My Chaste Heart, by the impulse of love, searches all ways to save all men from sin. My Son Jesus, through my Heart, wishes to impart to all men his divine blessings. I know many of you suffer many great difficulties because, in these last times, men no longer love or help one another but live with their hearts full of pride, falsehood, lies, intrigue, ambition, backbiting, pettiness, and many wrong things that are the consequences of living far from God.

My son, look at how much I suffered beside my Son Jesus and my Spouse the Blessed Virgin Mary! Like I have told you, I received from God the mission to be the guardian and protector of Jesus and Mary. My Heart was anguished because we did not live in the best of conditions in life, though I searched for a way to give a dignified life to the Son of the Most High.

The only means I had to bring home our daily bread was through my work as a carpenter. Work did not always have its adequate profit. Life had its problems, but I always trusted in Divine Providence. This was always our assistance for what was necessary for the survival of my beloved Son Jesus Christ.

My heart, would become distressed because I felt I was not giving my Son Jesus a dignified life. God permitted me to go through this so that I would grow to trust in his Divine Providence. The virtue of humility would adorn my soul and I would be an example to all men and workers, so that they would also fulfill their duties and work with patience and love.

My beloved son, to all who honor this Heart of mine and trust in me and in my intercession, I promise they will not be abandoned in their difficulties and in the trials of life. I will ask Our Lord to help them with his Divine Providence in their material and spiritual problems.

Mothers and fathers, consecrate yourselves to my Heart, likewise your families, and you will receive my help in your afflictions and problems. Just as I brought up the Son of the Most High in his holy laws, I will assist you with the upbringing and education of your children.

I will help all fathers and mothers that consecrate their children to me, to bring them up with love in the holy laws of God, so they may find the secure road to salvation.

Now I tell all men: consecrate yourselves to my Chaste Heart. Consecrate all to me: your lives, your families, your jobs. Consecrate all to me, because my Heart is the new font of graces that God concedes to all humanity. I extend my cloak over the whole world and all the Holy Church. Trust in me and you will receive all graces. I give you my blessing: in the name of the Father and of the Son and of the Holy Spirit. Amen.

March 7, 1998 – St. Joseph:

St. Joseph came in a leaf-green cloak and dark gray tunic. Our Blessed Mother came in a blue mantle and white dress with a white veil. The Child Jesus came in a light yellow tunic. St. Joseph held the right hand of the Child Jesus.

My beloved son, this night I, my Son Jesus and my spouse the Blessed Virgin, bless you in the name of the Father of the Son and of the Holy Spirit. My beloved son, my Son Jesus is very indignant with the sins of humanity.

He desires to pour his divine justice upon all men that do not want to repent and continue obstinately in their sins. Look, my son, I hold his right hand, preventing Him from pouring out his justice upon all humanity. I ask Him, through the graces of my Heart and for being worthy to live by his side, taking care of him with the love of a father in this world, and for Him having loved me with the love of a son, to not chastise the world for its crimes, but for all my little ones who honor and will honor this Chaste Heart of mine, should pour out his mercy upon the world.

How many sins are committed in the world, my son! It is necessary that men do much penance, that they repent of their errant attitudes, because God receives continued offenses from ungrateful men. Today there are so many outrages, the sacrilege and indifference by all men. It is because of this that so many calamities like war, hunger and disease occur and so many other sad things man has suffered because of man's rebellion against God.

God lets men follow their own paths to show them all, without him, they will never be happy. He lets men go through so much suffering, to also show them the consequences sin brings to their lives and so then the divine justice punishes humanity because of their obstinance in not being obedient to God's Will. Because of this, my beloved son, in these last times, humanity follows increasingly obstinate in their crimes, because what matters most for him are the pleasures of worldly things, rather than the love of God and his commandments. But God's justice is close at hand in a way never seen before and will come about suddenly upon the whole world.

So then, my son, tell all those that honor this Chaste Heart of mine they will receive the grace of my protection from all evils and dangers. For those who surrender to me will not be slaughtered by misfortunes, by wars, hunger, by diseases and other calamities, they will have my Heart as a refuge for their protection. Here, in my Heart, all will be protected against the divine justice in the days that will come. All who consecrate themselves to my Heart, honoring it, they will be looked upon by my Son Jesus with eyes of mercy, Jesus will pour out his love and will take to the glory of his Kingdom all those I put in my Heart. This is my message for tonight. I bless you: In the name of the Father and of the Son and of the Holy Spirit. Amen.

March 8, 1998 – St. Joseph:

St. Joseph was dressed in a dark maroon tunic and light maroon cloak, surrounded by twelve angels with large wings.

My beloved son, my Heart exults in joy by these encounters, I want to pour out these graces that the Lord has permitted me to give. I want, through my Heart, to lead all men to God. Here, in my Heart, all men are protected and through it they will understand the love of God in their lives.

My son, all those who propagate the devotion to my Heart, and practice it with love, have the certainty of having their names engraved on it just as my Son Jesus' cross and the "M" of Mary are engraved on it, as formed by wounds. This also applies for all priests whom I love with predilection. The priests who have a devotion to my Heart and spread it will have the grace of touching the most hardened hearts and convert obstinate sinners. That all may spread devotion to my Heart, it is God Himself who asks it. For all those who listen to my plea, I give my blessing.

You are to spread this devotion to all men, my beloved son, as you are designated by God to be the apostle of my Heart. Tell all of my love! Later I will come to speak to you about other things that will be very important for the salvation of many souls. God has entrusted you with a great mission – trust in me and you will know how to truly realize it. I give you my blessing: in the name of the Father of the Son and of the Holy Spirit. Amen.

March 9, 1998 – St. Joseph, Our Lady, and the Child Jesus: St. Joseph came, in a burgundy cloak and white tunic, with Our Lady, in a blue mantle and white dress. The Child Jesus, all in white, was sitting on St. Joseph's lap.

My beloved son, this night I, my Son Jesus, and my Most Chaste Spouse St. Joseph, bless the whole world. I ask you to listen and to live the holy messages of God.

Convert. Continue to pray the holy Rosary every day and, particularly, beloved son, the seven Apostles' Creeds, because here in the Amazon there will be a great loss of faith. It is because of this I ask you to always pray the seven Creeds, since many will lose their faith and abandon the Holy Church in the difficult moments to come. I, your Mother, ask you to continue to pray to prevent that great danger and those difficult days during which many will suffer.

All who honor the Most Chaste Heart of St. Joseph will benefit with my maternal presence in their lives in a special way.

I will be at the side of each son and daughter of mine, helping and comforting them with a Mothers' Heart, just as I helped and comforted my Most Chaste Spouse Joseph in this world. To those who ask of his Heart with trust, I promise to intercede before the Eternal Father, my Divine Son Jesus, and the Holy Spirit. I will obtain for them, from God, the grace to reach perfect sanctity in the virtues of St. Joseph, this way reaching the perfect love in which he lived. Men will learn to love my Son Jesus and myself with the same love as my Most Chaste Spouse Joseph, receiving the most pure love from our Hearts.

My Son Jesus, my Chaste Spouse Joseph, and I are at your side. Fear nothing, because our hearts will protect you always. I give you my blessing: in the name of the Father and of the Son and of the Holy Spirit. Amen.

At the end of this message the Holy Family gave their blessing and as they were rising to Heaven, Our Lady said: "*In the end our united Hearts will triumph!*"

Simply put, these nine messages regarding God's manifest will and desire for devotion of and Consecration to the Most Chaste Heart of St. Joseph by humanity in its present ubiquitous state of moral degeneration, disaster and war, constitute one of the greatest series of prophetic messages regarding St. Joseph in the history of the Catholic Church.

On July 16, 2001, Edson was in Italy on the feast of Our Lady of Mt. Carmel, and was quite unaware that this day happened to be the 750th anniversary of the revelation of the Brown Scapular to the St. Simon Stock, 13th century Minster General of the Carmelite Order. After speaking to a youth group in the city of Sciacca, Edson received this prodigious vision of the Holy Family, during which the "Scapular of St. Joseph" was revealed. Our Lady gives the specific  instruction to have this scapular made and worn by everyone as a manifestation of the love that St. Joseph deserves, and for the protection and sanctification of God through St. Joseph's intercession:

Edson: I was in the city of Sciacca, in the province of Agrigento, Sicily, Italy, visiting a local youth group. During the afternoon, after praying the rosary and giving my testimony at the church of Our Lady of the Rosary of Fatima (which is run by the Capuchin Franciscan Friars), I had a vision of the Holy Family in front of the people who were present.

In this apparition, Our Lady gave me a message and said:

> *Pay attention to what I will show you. Have a scapular made according to what you shall see. That will be the scapular of St. Joseph. My Son Jesus and I wish everyone to wear it with love and faith, in deep honor of my spouse Joseph, as he deserves. Those who bear this scapular shall receive the protection from God, through the Most Chaste Heart and sheltering mantle of St. Joseph, as well as many blessings necessary for their salvation and saintliness.*

Over the image of the Holy Family, I saw the following phrase written in golden letters: "**Most Chaste Heart of St. Joseph**" and below: "**Be the guardian of our family!**"

Edson: Soon afterwards, this vision disappeared, to give place to three illumined and glowing hearts. There were two rays of light coming from the Heart of Jesus and going towards the Immaculate Heart of Mary and to the Most

Chaste Heart of St. Joseph, and from them, those rays departed and were directed to the world. Above those Hearts, these words appeared, written in golden letters: "**Jesus, Mary and Joseph,**" and under them: "**I love Thee, save souls!**"

Following this vision, Our Lady reappeared carrying Her child Jesus, next to St. Joseph. Together, they blessed every present person and disappeared amidst the beautiful light that surrounded them. I did not know that, on this day, the Carmelite order and the Church around the world celebrated the 750th year in which Our Lady entrusted the scapular to St. Simon Stock. This was a special day for the Carmelites, a great event for the order of the Carmelites, and the day in which Jesus and Our Lady asked the Church and the world for the scapular of St. Joseph, as a special protection for the families around the world.

This vision of July 16, 2001 was actually the second time that Edson had received a vision of the Scapular of St. Joseph. The first time was on July 14, 2000 when Edson was in England and visiting the Sanctuary of Our Lady of Mount Carmel in Aylesfort, in the same place where the Most Holy Virgin had appeared to St. Simon Stock and revealed to him the traditional Brown Scapular. Only during this second vision did Edson receive the instruction to have the Scapular of St. Joseph and distributed worldwide.

The revelation of March 29, 2002 provides us with yet another truly historic contribution to devotion to St. Joseph. St. Joseph appeared to Edson while the visionary was praying a prayer to St. Joseph which he had been praying for some time. St. Joseph gave Edson the instruction to "spread this prayer to the whole world." This mystical exchange with St. Joseph left Edson with the consequent inspiration to enumerate the six principle ways in which to give proper veneration to the Most Chaste Heart of St. Joseph:

This prayer, the "Hail Joseph" appears below, along with Edson's description of the momentous supernatural event:

Hail Joseph

> *"Hail Joseph, Son of David, just and virginal man,*
> *Wisdom is with you;*
> *blessed are you among all men, and blessed is Jesus,*
> *the fruit of Mary, your faithful Spouse.*
>
> *Holy Joseph, worthy Father and*
> *Protector of Jesus Christ and of Holy Church,*
> *pray for us sinners and obtain for us from God Divine Wisdom,*
> *now and at the hour of our death. Amen."*

Edson: In the morning of March 29, 2002, while I was praying, St. Joseph appeared. He was very handsome and he showed me his Most Chaste Heart. He appeared while I was praying the prayer (Hail Joseph), which I had been praying in his honor for some time. Looking at me with a warm smile, he gave me the following message:

> *Spread this prayer to the whole world. Through this prayer God wishes my name to be more known and loved. He also wants to bestow a lot of graces through it upon those who will honor me by praying it. Those who will pray this prayer will be given many graces from Heaven. Through it, I will be often invoked by the whole world, and I will be able, by my loved and honorable heart, to grant a lot of graces to sinners who are in need of divine help. It is important that this prayer be made known to everyone. May it reach everywhere, so all people can enjoy the goodness of God through it. This is His Most Holy Will that I am revealing to you right now.*

I felt overwhelmed by God's presence, and I understood many things which were revealed to my heart about this devotion and about my future life and my mission. I am not worthy to receive such wonderful graces, and I deeply thanked God to have been chosen to present the Most Chaste Heart of St. Joseph to the entire world. Who am I for this mission?

Nothing, but I want to continue to be nothing so that God can do everything. Therefore, I understood that there are six different ways to honor the Heart of St. Joseph:

1. **The Image of the Most Chaste Heart of St. Joseph:** presented during the Apparition of December 25, 1996, in which Jesus and Our Lady revealed the Heart of St. Joseph to the world.

2. **The Feast of the Most Chaste Heart of St. Joseph:** as requested by Jesus during the Apparition of June 6, 1997: *"I wish the first Wednesday after the Feast of My Sacred Heart and the Immaculate Heart of Mary be the Feast of the Most Chaste Heart of St. Joseph."*

3. **The Chaplet of the Seven Sorrows and Seven Joys of St. Joseph:** which now can be prayed with the prayer that St. Joseph gave during the Apparition of March 29, 2002.

4. **The Scapular of St. Joseph:** The Scapular is a sign of protection and devotion to the Heart of St. Joseph, who wants to lead us to God and to holiness, emphasizing his virtues of purity, obedience, silence, and humility, and igniting the flame of faith and love for Jesus and for the Holy Virgin Mary. St. Joseph will protect those wearing the Scapular as his property and will bestow innumerable graces through his Chaste Heart upon

those who will be tempted against purity, and will protect them against the attacks by the Devil and each evil spirit. Especially young people should wear this Scapular, as they are most attacked by the Devil. Parents should recommend it to their children, since St. Joseph offers his help and protection, as he guided and protected Jesus on earth.

5. **The Spreading of Devotion to the Heart of St. Joseph**: associated with good deeds of charity in favor of the most needy, especially of the sick and dying, as St. Joseph requested in his promises in March 1998.

6. **First Wednesdays:** should be remembered as days of special graces where St. Joseph pours out torrents of extraordinary graces upon all those who appeal to his intercession, honoring his Most Chaste Heart. Jesus himself promised that these faithful servants will enjoy great glory in Heaven which, on the other hand, will not be given to those who will not honor him as He asked.*

As far back as October, 1996, Edson received a private message from St. Joseph (only for himself) about the "Holy Cloak of St. Joseph." He understood that he should pray the Holy Cloak, together with devotion to the Scapular. You can find a recent edition of the traditional Holy Cloak of St. Joseph prayer in Appendix II.

These Itapiranga revelations regarding the Most Chaste Heart of St. Joseph, the Promises associated with Consecration to his Heart, the Scapular of St. Joseph, the Hail Joseph Prayer, and the devotion to the Holy Cloak all represent truly history-making contributions to authentic Catholic devotion to the Guardian of the Redeemer and Virginal Spouse of the Immaculate Mother of God.

God's timing is always perfect, and it is God's will that this new generosity of devotion to St. Joseph come *right now*, when the Church and the world have dire need for the full blown powerful intercession of the Patron of the Universal Church. May St. Joseph's Most Chaste Heart give each of us the wisdom and grace to personally implement today these salvific and life-changing devotions given us by God for our personal, family, Church and global protection and sanctification amidst the omnipresent forms of moral, social, and worldwide challenges that likewise are revealed to be "coming soon."

* Special thanks goes to Michael Journal for the translation of the messages of March 1-9, 1998 and the accompanying commentary (*www.michaeljournal.org*).

CHAPTER V

ITAPIRANGA AND THE 21ST CENTURY

As the celestial messages from the Queen of the Rosary and of Peace continue into the 21st century, we see a profound blending of themes which include both words of warning, but also the promise of ultimate victory with the eventual Triumph of Mary's Immaculate Heart and the restoration of world peace. As Our Lady puts it, *"The world will be renewed and a new dawn of peace shall take place."*

The messages of 2001, while reiterating key themes from the past, will also accentuate the importance of Itapiranga in the plan of God for the Amazon region and for all humanity: *"Itapiranga, Itapiranga, a place so simple and hidden, but so exceptional to the eyes of God."* Due to their importance in setting out the themes for the new millennium, all 2001 messages (except for the July 16, 2001 message concerning the Three Hearts and St. Joseph just examined in the last chapter) will be presented here.

The Queen of Peace begins the year with one of her first references to the future fruits of responding to her messages: a renewal of peace through the Triumph of her Immaculate Heart (January 1, 2001):

Peace be with you!

Dear children, I am the Mother of God and I bless each one of you. O how I love you! Today I bless you with a blessing of peace. I am the Queen of Peace. God, Our Lord, has sent Me from Heaven to bestow upon you His holy blessings and His message of peace. I come down from Heaven because God loves you.

Little children, a new year begins. How joyful I am to see that you start this new year with God. Jesus is granting a special blessing for your families. Jesus can solve even the most difficult problems, if you trust Him.

My Immaculate Heart is overjoyed for seeing you here. Today I bless the whole world. It was here, dear children, at this place, that your Celestial Mother appeared for the first time. And it is right here, that I turn to tell you once more: pray, pray!

I bless the entire Holy Church. I bless in a special way the local church of Amazonas. I bless all the missionaries of My Son Jesus. It is necessary to evangelize for there are many hearts that are still closed to God. The word of God must reach out to the most remote places because the word of God means life to all My children.

Priests, priests, priests be faithful to God. Priests, so dear to My heart, love God. Be united to Him. Bring His love to all the faithful. I invite you to be saints. Do not be a cause of sorrow for My Heart.

My beloved children who are present here today, pray with me again for the priests…

Our Lady prayed one "Our Father" and one "Glory Be" for the priests.

The one who is united to God shall fear nothing. Behold that the world will be renewed and a new dawn of peace will arrive. The battle between good and evil is coming to an end. I want you united to me in the day of My triumph, at the triumph of My Immaculate Heart. Whoever consecrates himself/herself to Me, I will be his/her intercessor before My Son Jesus. I bless you again: in the name of the Father, the Son, and the Holy Spirit. Amen!

I wait for you at Itapiranga, because that is the place chosen by my Immaculate Heart for the entire people of Amazonas. With the zeal of your love and your dedication build the Sanctuary of God here in the Amazonas. Be zealous for the work of God. Itapiranga is the source of grace and love of God for all my children. From Itapiranga the Lord shines His light to the whole world.

Itapiranga, Itapiranga, a place so simples and hidden, but so huge to the eyes of God. I thank you again for your presence, My children. Remain with God's peace, in the name of the Father, the Son and the Holy Spirit. Amen!

January 23, 2001 brings a renewed call for praying for families in the midst of the present societal attacks on true marriage and family life. Our Lady of Itapiranga also prophecies "great changes" coming:

Whoever loves and serves the Lord is always heard in his prayers. The Lord always hears and responds to the ones who yearn for His love. Pray with Me for all the families...

The Virgin prayed three "Glory Be's" for the families.

Dear children, continue to love the Lord and to offer Him your love. I come from heaven to bless you as your Mother.

My Son Jesus sends Me here to grant you His blessings and grace. Pray with love! Pray each time more, so that the grace of God comes down from Heaven ever more.

This will be the year of great changes for all humanity. Be prepared! The Lord is returning once more upon the earth to gather His people together. The ones who belong to the Lord shall fear nothing.

I bless you with My Maternal blessing, a Mother's blessing: in the name of the Father, the Son, and the Holy Spirit. Amen! Remain with the peace of Jesus!

This January 25, 2001 message from St. Michael the Archangel conveys the urgent summons for obedience to Our Lady's messages:

Jesus and the Virgin have sent me here. I am St. Michael the Archangel!

The Queen of Peace is being sent to the entire world to invite Her children to conversion, but there are still many who do not heed Her messages or believe in her apparitions.

Pray truly with your hearts. Open your hearts to God. The Queen of Peace is demanding obedience from each one of you. Whoever does not obey will suffer greatly yet, for the ones who do not listen to the voice from Heaven do not please God. If you are obedient you will find salvation. The Mother of God blesses you, together with Her Son Jesus, Our Lord. I bless you in His name and in the name of the Holy Trinity: in the name of the Father, the Son and the Holy Spirit. Amen!

Our Lady calls us to "open our hearts" through prayer to the Holy Spirit, her divine spouse, in order to obtain the spiritual fruit of peace, as well as a personal message of encouragement for someone in the crowd (January 30, 2001):

Peace be with you!

Dear children, I am your celestial Mother and I love you.

I want to tell you tonight that God loves you and blesses you, bestowing upon you many blessings. Open up your hearts to Him and receive His message of love. If you do this, peace will enter your hearts, remain with you, and it will come to your families.

Pray to the Holy Spirit. He will guide you, showing you the way of the truth, and your mission. I love you, and as a mother I desire to help you fulfill God's will. Pray always, because within your prayers God will reveal Himself, as well as His love. I bless you all: in the name of the Father, the Son, and the Holy Spirit. Amen!

Edson: The Virgin issued one message to a person:

Tell my son not to worry. I love him the way he is and I know his capabilities. If he opens himself to love he may comprehend what I desire from him. What I desire is that whatever he does he does with love, even if he is not able of doing everything, that all his intentions be based on love. It is God who sanctifies and perfects everything. Let God lead everything.

Edson: Our Lady asks the question, "Do you know what conversion means?" and then offers the answer in this January 31ˢᵗ message:

> *Dear children, I am the Mother of Jesus, and tonight I wish to thank you for your prayers. The Lord blesses you and invites you to conversion. Do you know what conversion means? Conversion is to live a new life with God, totally renewed, freed from all evil and from every sinful attitude. Conversion is to live a life with love and forgiveness with each other, truly loving each other in Jesus, My Beloved Son. Conversion is to live a life of respect towards your brethren, for everyone is a temple of the Holy Spirit and a precious part of Him.*
>
> *For that reason, My dear children, bear a great love and respect for all My children, hence you shall make God and Myself happy. Pray always more and your lives will be renewed by the Love of God. I bless you all: in the name of the Father, the Son, and the Holy Spirit. Amen!*

St. Joseph delivers this January 31, 2001 message concerning the powerful intercession of his Most Chaste Heart, the imperative for priests to respect the works of God, and for continued prayer to the Holy Spirit:

> *My dear son, peace be with you and with everyone.*
>
> *Today, I pour upon all humanity the graces from my Most Chaste Heart. God wishes that all mankind benefits from His grace, through the intercession of My Heart to Him.*
>
> *I love humankind and I desire that it comes closer to Me, because I wish to help humanity to walk always towards heaven, to God.*

You are to tell your bishop to see to it well, pondering with love and discernment what Jesus and the Most Holy Virgin, My spouse, have done at Itapiranga.

Itapiranga is a great grace and a gift from God for the people of Amazonas and for the entire humanity. Itapiranga must be better known by the children of God, for the message that was transmitted there will be for the salvation of many souls.

The priests must know how to respect the works of God. How saddened God becomes when the priests, without knowing about the messages and apparition, criticize them and ridicule them. Those are worse than the scribes and Pharisees. Those are the "Thomas" of our days.

Priests, the Lord calls you to a deep reflection on your attitudes. Be careful and zealous for the work of the Lord, because what He does is for the salvation of your people, the same ones left aside, and abandoned by many of you, who with a bad example, did not fulfill your vocation and ministry as one should.

Pray to the Holy Spirit, He will help you to be faithful to your vocation. Ask for My aid and I will come to assist you. I bless all of you: in the name of the Father, the Son and the Holy Spirit. Amen!

The Feast of the Presentation of the Lord (February 2, 2001) brings the repeated exhortation to pray, coupled with a strong warning of "woe" for those who do not take her Itapiranga messages seriously. Our Lady reiterates, "I do not speak out as a joke:"

Peace be with you!

Dear children, convert yourselves and live a holy and prayerful life.

The Lord once more calls you, through Me, to a change in your lives. Be faithful to your Christian commitments as spouses, children, brothers and sisters, and as parents. Do not allow Satan to destroy your families and the peace God granted them through His presence.

Many times when I see that you do not listen to me, I become concerned. My words are not a joke. Take a concrete decision to convert because your time is running out. Woe to those who do not heed my messages and my apparitions and waste the grace from Heaven. I pray for your conversion and so you decide for the path that leads to God.

I bless all My ill children, and I pray asking the blessing of God and His grace over all of them. Pray, pray, pray and you shall become the most beautiful flowers in the garden of God, watered by His Holy Love. I bless you all: in the name of the Father, the Son, and the Holy Spirit. Amen!

May 13, 2001 commemorates the anniversary of Our Lady's first apparition at Fatima. As the "Lady of the Rosary and Mother of all humanity" she repeats the Fatima call for Rosary and penance, along with admonitions to those, particularly among her "predilected" or particularly beloved clergy who are not listening to these critical messages of Itapiranga—vital communications for the Amazon region and beyond. She also offers a special blessing for the Holy Father:

Peace be with you!

Dear children I am the Lady of the Rosary and Mother of all humanity.

Pray the Rosary. Your prayers are still important for the salvation of many souls. Do penance. Many do not offer sacrifice for the salvation of their brethren. I invite you again: fast. Do not disregard fasting. It will be very important, My children. Pay attention to what I tell you.

The Creator allowed me to speak to you again. Be obedient to God. Ask for God's mercy every day for this world, for Brazil and for the Amazonas.

Amazonas! Amazonas! How much sufferings I foresee if you do not heed my appeal!

Again I warn My favorite sons. Why do you not listen to Me? Why do you not heed My appeals, My favorite little children, priests of my Immaculate Heart? Do you not love your mother? I love you very much, and for that reason I am here to help you, My priest sons.

I came to Amazonas to aid all of My children: bishops, priests, consecrated ones, the faithful, and all those who need My Maternal help. I did not come down from Heaven for fun, but for a very serious reason: to invite you to love, peace, unity and obedience to the Commandments of God, and to His Holy Church.

At this moment, I pour down from Heaven a shower of blessings. The Creator at this moment looks at each one of you and blesses you. Turn your crosses and sorrows into blessings for the salvation of many souls, offering them up to God so that He will sanctify them. Do not be afraid. Do not have fear in face of tribulations. God is with you.

From here I bless My favorite son, the Holy Father, the pope. Today the whole world is united in continuous and fervent prayer. Many of My children are praying in Fatima. Today Francisco and Jacinta are by My side, blessing you and praying for you to God. They have suffered and were courageous, never renounced their faith and their love to this Mother who loves humankind.

My children, there are too many sins and offenses against God. Poor sinful humankind! But you can help her if you pray, sacrificing yourselves offering God reparations and sacrifices for the conversion of sous, as my 3 little shepherds did.

Behold, the Lord will renew everything. The world will be renewed and the love of God shall reign in every heart, in the life of all of My children. Blessed are those who open their hearts to God. The Lord has prepared many blessings for those who listen to and live His Word. Remain with the peace of God, take it to every man and woman, for the world will be renewed so that every man and woman may live as true brothers and sisters.

I am the star who precedes the second coming of the Lord. I am the One who shall crush the head of the serpent. I am your Mother and the Queen of Heaven and of earth. For all of you My maternal love and blessing: in the name of the Father, the Son and of the Holy Spirit. Amen!

The June 23, 2001 apparition on the Feast of the Immaculate Heart of Mary revealed the "Queen of all Hearts" wearing a crown of white roses, accompanied by two angels. She was particularly happy due to the graces being showered upon the world through her Immaculate Heart on this day:

Edson: I saw the Most Holy Virgin at the Our Lady of Remedies Church, in Manaus. She was so beautiful. This apparition took place during communion, after I received communion. The Virgin appeared in front of the altar, when Father James was distributing communion to the faithful. She was a little over him, in the air. Her mantle was large, and there were two angels holding it behind the Virgin. It was silvery white, and in its inner side it was blue. Her tunic was white, in the same style of the mantle. She was showing Her Immaculate Heart which was of a very bright red color, as I had never seen before, and from it emanated intense rays of light over everyone in the church. I also understood that those rays were designated for the whole world.

Edson: On the Virgin's head there was a crown of white roses. She was very happy and she told me:

> *The Lord has sent me here so that the humankind will be benefitted by His grace, through My Immaculate Heart and My maternal blessing.*

> *Today the world and the Church are receiving My blessings and grace that comes from the Lord and are transmitted through the rays of light that depart from My maternal heart.*

Edson: Looking at Father James, the Virgin approached him delicately and put her right hand over him. She inclined her head and as a sign of respect to Jesus in the Eucharist and to the priest who was distributing the hosts to the faithful, for he is a minister of God. The Virgin cheerfully asked me to tell the priest:

> *Tell My favorite son that My Immaculate Heart is joyful and I am thankful for the procession he permitted in honor of this heart of mine, pure and virginal, that God*

*has granted Me, enriching it with His love, grace and
blessings, being his vase of virtues, of grace and protection
to those who approach Him with Love, devotion and
respect. The Lord God, rich in love and mercy, and
desirous to grant salvation to the souls, aiding them by
a simple gesture of love done to His Most Holy Mother,
showing Himself generous and prone to distribute His
gifts and grace ever more to all His children.*

It was at this moment that the Mother of God, slowly moving
down from above, touched the church's floor with her feet,
where the priest had distributed the hosts, right at the center.
Since the beginning of the apparition, I have realized that the
Virgin did not have the cloud that was always beneath her
feet, and so I understood the reason for her act. She remained
silent for a moment, looking at me and at everyone in the
church. I said to myself:

"Forgive me, Mother, for not kneeling, if I do that I will attract
everyone's attention, and they may notice that something is
taking place. For that reason I remained seated!!"

She smiled as if listening to me. Afterwards, I thought to myself:

"How I wish I could go where You are and kiss your feet that
are now touching this floor, and also kiss the place where you
are stepping on, for it seems so unclean for her holy, beautiful
and perfect feet to tread on!"

She smiled at me even more and said:

*Every spot in the house of God is holy and worthy of
respect. For God everything is clean and perfect, for
wherever God is everything is sanctified by His presence.
Real dirt only enters His house, His Holy Temple, when
men come to Church with their rotten souls, decayed by
the most horrible sins, and go many times toward the holy*

altar of the Lord, offending Him with the most horrible transgressions and sacrileges committed against Him in the Holy Eucharist. This is the only way that filthiness enters the House of God.

Afterwards she extended her hands over the assembly, as if she were praying for her children in silence. Then, lowering her hands, she looked at me again, saying:

It is here, in this most sublime moment, of the union of God with the souls, during the Eucharist, that many miracles take place and many hearts are renewed through His love. This is the moment in which the Lord heals many people from spiritual blindness, from their cold and hardened hearts, granting them many spiritual blessings, as well as many physical blessings for their infirmities.

I am the Queen of all hearts, I desire to have all the hearts warmed here, inside My Immaculate Heart, through the flames of My love, so that those hearts will ever be more on fire to have a greater and more profound love for the Lord.

I saw many small hearts entering the heart of Our Lady and becoming beautiful, radiant, with a similar vivid color as that of her Immaculate Heart. The Virgin continued:

Here in this place where I have appeared, the Lord wishes to heal many souls with His Love, offering to all My children the remedy to all their infirmities, through the Eucharist that was worthily and saintly received, and through the graces that flow from My Immaculate Heart, that your Celestial Mother deigned to reveal so lovingly and maternally to all her children and as a strong and efficacious means to obtain the blessings from God. To all of you My maternal blessing, from the bottom of my

Heart: in the name of the Father, the Son, and the Holy
Spirit. Amen!

I also saw the Most Chaste Heart of St. Joseph, above the
Virgin, very luminous and beautiful, surrounded by white
lilies. I understood that the Virgin, during the feast of her
Immaculate Heart, was requesting that the Church recognizes
the feast day to honor St. Joseph's heart and devotion to him.

Wednesday, June 27th was the anticipated feast of the Most
Chaste heart of St. Joseph during 2001. St. Joseph conveyed
touching words, of Edson's selection, by St. Joseph himself,
to spread devotion to His Most Chaste Heart and how as
a result his pure Heart will become even more resplendent
throughout the world:

> *Dear son, God has assigned to you a great mission:*
> *to transmit the devotion to my Most Chaste Heart*
> *to the world. What an honorable, beautiful and*
> *wonderful mission!*
>
> *Amongst so many people, I have chosen you, even in the*
> *past, when you were away from the Lord, when you were*
> *not His yet and you followed your own paths. But I asked*
> *the Lord that He would look down upon the one I had*
> *chosen in Amazonas, as His family.*
>
> *Do you know why I wished to appear in a home to reveal*
> *My heart to the world? Because I wish to show the world*
> *how much I love the families and how much they are*
> *important to God, for I was the chief of the Holy Family*
> *and I still am.*
>
> *The Lord has granted me a great glory. He gave Me the*
> *grace of having a chaste and virginal heart. He created*

a holy heart for me, where He could place His grace. Truly, my Most Chaste Heart is full of the most abundant blessings from the Lord, filled with virtues and blessings.

I am the righteous one of the Lord. He who has always grown in divine virtues, and in the grace of God. Those who call upon My holy name, the most worthy and holy name that the Lord has dedicated to Me, and called Me by, I promise the abundance of my celestial blessings, and My protection against all the iniquities from hell, and the immediate deliverance, in all dangers and afflictions.

You saw today how much I love you and wish your wellbeing. Today many have witnessed the protection I grant you. Fear Nothing. The enemy cannot harm you, for I accompany you.

Today, through your prayers and the prayers of your brothers and sisters, much illness that the Enemy wished to unleash against the church of Amazonas and the souls were destroyed. Whatever he had planned will not take place and the grace of God will come down upon you and your families.

My heart will shine ever more in the world.

At that moment I saw in many parts of the world people doing processions, great celebration and works in honor of the Most Chaste Heart of St. Joseph. Right then I saw the globe representing the world. In it, small lights started to appear on each continent, shining in many places until there were many lights shining intensely in many places. I heard the voice of St. Joseph saying:

It shall be that way!

I understood that where the lights were glowing those would be the places where the heart of St. Joseph would be honored, and where his devotion would reach. As I saw in my vision, it will reach every place in the world. St. Joseph continued, saying:

> *Hence my children may benefit from the grace of God. I thank you for your presence and for the love you have offered to me. To all of you my paternal blessing and protection: in the name of the Father, the Son, and the Holy Spirit. Amen!*

This July 7, 2001 message was received while Edson was in Assisi, Italy. Our Lady specifically alludes to St. Francis in her message calling for ongoing fidelity to this heavenly mission:

> *Today God blesses you. God makes Himself present in the union of one with another. He fulfills His work as He pleases and takes it forward. He never abandons His people, His children, those who serve Him with an open heart, and trust Him.*
>
> *The littlest ones are those who can receive everything from His merciful heart. The little ones include all those who are humble, who have no pretensions, those who dedicate themselves confidently to His loving plan, who do not doubt His kindness and never allow pride and conceit to approach their hearts. It means those who, in their nothingness, allow God to do everything.*
>
> *I love you like a mother and I offer you My aid, for God has allowed Me to favor you. Bring the work of God forward, do not get discouraged. I thank you for your disposition My child. You will always go ahead, taking my messages and fulfilling the Lord's will. You shall still visit other*

places, like Francisco* did. I bless all of you: in the name of the Father, of the Son, and of the Holy Spirit. Amen!

*St. Francis of Assisi

"I love you and I bring you to my Immaculate Heart," Our Lady expresses in this July 8, 2001 message. She calls us to testify to the love of God to our "brothers and sisters" and thus to spread God's kingdom on earth:

> *My dear children, I love you and I place you in My Immaculate Heart. Pray, because with prayer your hearts will be filled with God`s love and He will bring you peace. Jesus loves you. I give you today His peace, a peace that He allows Me to grant you, because I am the Queen of Peace.*
>
> *Belong to Jesus and give testimony of the love of God to your brothers and sisters – by doing so you will help God's kingdom expand to the whole world and in their lives.*
>
> *The Lord is happy for your presence and prayers. As your mother I bless you: in the name of the Father, of the Son, and of the Holy Spirit. Amen!*

The following message (July 9, 2001) identifies the Itapiranga message as coming from the "deep mysteries" of Our Lady's Immaculate Heart. She also confirms to Edson that he was specifically chosen for this great work:

> *Beloved son, I wish to give you My message... that came as a great grace to My Church, because it has emerged from the deep mysteries of My Heart, which were concealed in My secret, and now it is revealed ever more to the Church.*

Do not worry about what you are to say. It is I who will speak. You must only write my message. Give thanks to the Father for everything that you have learned and heard from My mouth, for He desires everyone to be dressed by the Spirit of Truth.

The Holy Trinity is with you and everyone. Today I address you. Do you understand all that is currently happening? Those are great things, My son. You have not evaluated these events yet, but you will understand My plans ever more.

Edson, you were called by Me. Again I tell you, as I said at the beginning of your journey: (*) do not reject the gift that was given you, the grace I have granted you, when the elderly assembly put their hands over you, receiving you as a prophecy. Do you remember that moment?

I was then preparing you for everything that is happening now. Be faithful. Do not be afraid!

All I want is confidence, for only thus I may use you for My work, in My way. Courage. Take heart. Forward. It is time to leave the deep sleep, to be awake and attentive when the Lord comes and calls you to follow Him. I bless all of you: in the name of the Father, of the Son, and the Holy Spirit. Amen!

*1 Timothy 4, 14-15

Given in Palermo, Italy, the message of July 11, 2001 calls us to be "builders of peace" at the service of the Queen of Peace:

Peace be with you!

My beloved children, I am Jesus' Mother and the Queen of Peace. Today I bless you and pour My love upon you. I never abandon you. God sent Me here to invite you to live in peace and in love among yourselves.

Be builders of peace. Help those most in need. Be an example of love and truth. If you do not love your brethren and do not give you help to your neighbors, you will not be doing anything. Do not allow selfishness and self-indulgence to take over your hearts. Give yourself totally for the happiness of your most suffering brothers.

I carry you in My Immaculate Heart. Here in My Heart you will receive many graces from the Lord. I am happy for your presence and for your prayers.

Today I am also blessing your families. Be faithful to God. Be obedient to the Church. Be true apostles of My Son Jesus. I bless My favorite children. I bless all of you: in the name of the Father, of the Son, and the Holy Spirit. Amen!

As a special message to the youth, the July 12, 2001 communication instructs today's young people to "be the children of God, not children of the darkness":

Peace be with you!

Dear children, I am the Queen of Peace. I invite you to prayer and conversion. Pray, pray and pray. Through prayer you will find peace and joy from God and thus your lives will be transformed. As your Mother I bless you and I place you inside My Heart.

*My dear youth, thank you for your presence. Today I bless
you in a special manner and I present you to Jesus. You are
important to God. In order for you to understand My call:
pray! Do not let the goodness in you be destroyed by sin.
Be the children of God, not children of darkness. Each one
of you is special to My Heart. If you dedicate your hearts
to Me I can offer them to Jesus. Pray for your families and
for the youth of the whole world.*

*If you pray, many will find God's light and will be saved.
May prayer be always part of your life. Jesus has sent me
here to grant you His grace and His love.*

*Do not fear anything because God is always with you and
protects you. If you heed My plea, you will be concurring
to the good and the peace of this world.*

*Listen to Me! Listen to Me! Listen to Me! I speak to you
as a loving and kind mother, because all of you are My
children. I send you My kiss of love and My blessing:
in the name of the Father, of the Son, and of the Holy
Spirit. Amen.*

This July 13, 2001 revelation comes on the anniversary of
the third 1917 Fatima message. Here, Our Lady asks for
perseverance in witnessing to the plan of God, and for special
prayer for priests:

Peace be with you!

*My children, continue to follow the path designed by God.
God loves you so, and His great love encompasses you at
this moment.*

*The Lord sends His light and blessing from heaven. May
each one of you who are here be true witness of love.*

Amen, amen, amen. Love transforms and sanctifies you. With love, everything that does not bring you peace will be destroyed. When you love, you are always more united to God, who is true love.

Thank you for your presence. Tomorrow I will return with My Son Jesus, Who will come to bless you. Pray for the Church and for My sons, the priests. Those who pray for the priests have God´s blessing. I bless all of you: in the name of the Father, of the Son, and the Holy Spirit. Amen!

"*I am the Queen of Heaven and Earth and your Mother*" Our Lady declares (July 14, 2001). She encourages humility and simplicity in seeking the Kingdom of God:

Peace be with you!

Dear children, I am the Queen of Heaven and Earth, and your Mother.

Today I bless you, together with My Son Jesus, Who is here at my side.

Jesus loves you so and desires from you obedience and humility. Be humble and simple, in order for you to deserve the kingdom of Heaven. Do not fear anything, for I am here to protect you and place you under my Immaculate mantle.

Be children of prayer and faith. Increase your faith by daily asking God for it in your prayers. I thank you for your presence and for the love you have for Me and for My Son Jesus. I bless all of you: in the name of the Father, of the Son, and the Holy Spirit. Amen!

July 15, 2001 brings a message conveying that Our Mother is "happy" for the presence of those in attendance, and promises a "great reward" for those who persevere in striving to work for God's kingdom unto heaven:

> *Peace be with you!*
>
> *Dear children, I am happy for your presence. I love you so and desire your salvation. Continue to pray the holy Rosary. Know that your prayers are helping Me to establish My plans of conversion.*
>
> *Today I grant you all my love, so that you may transmit it to all My children.*
>
> *Strive for the construction of God's kingdom on earth, so that you may one day deserve the Kingdom of heaven. Heaven waits for you!*
>
> *Each time, God's work is being fulfilled. In Heaven, you shall receive a great reward from God. Do not be discouraged.*
>
> *Be truthful, obedient, and humble, because humility pleases My Maternal Heart.*
>
> *Give thanks to God for everything that He is doing. I bless you and keep you within My heart. I bless all of you: in the name of the Father, of the Son, and the Holy Spirit. Amen!*

Our Lady informs us that many souls are about to be lost, and therefore sounds the urgent need for global conversion (July 17, 2001 message):

Peace be with you!

Dear children, I am the Blessed Virgin Mary, Mother of Jesus.

Pray the holy Rosary every day, and thus God's blessings will be poured down upon you and your family. I love you so much and I am here because I wish to grant you My Maternal Love.

The world needs to convert: I say it again! How many souls risk being eternally lost. Help Me, My little ones, help Me with your prayers, so that the world may find the light of God and convert.

I am always at your side and never abandon you. Thank you for the prayers that you have offered to God and to Me for the salvation of souls. Do penances and sacrifices always for the salvation of souls. I bless all of you: in the name of the Father, of the Son, and the Holy Spirit. Amen

This July 20, 2001 message requests that our "hearts be always focused on Heaven" and encourages us to faithfully pray the Rosary and Eucharistic Adoration so that Our Lady can continue to save souls through our prayers. She also explains the great efficacy of the "O My Jesus" prayer revealed at Fatima:

Peace be with you!

Dear children, I am your Mother and I love you so much. Abundant goodness I desire for you and your families. My Immaculate Heart is joyful, because your prayers are helping Me to save many souls.

Always pray the holy Rosary. If you offer Me your prayers with love and devotion, then I can intercede with my Son Jesus, so that they will be transformed into blessings and graces for you, for your families and for the whole world.

Jesus always waits for you in the Tabernacle and in the church. He loves you very much and desires your salvation. He, the Omnipotent and Holy one, the one Who is, Who was, and is to come, shall renew the entire world with the blazing fire of love that comes from His Sacred Heart.

How many wonders My Son Jesus is performing in the world! My little children, do not ever think that My apparitions in this world are of little importance, because if they did not happen, as they do now, many souls would have already been eternally suffering in hell – but because of My apparitions, they have found light and divine grace and were saved, for they have lived according to My appeals.

When I appeared to My little Portuguese shepherds at Fatima, I taught them this little prayer:

Oh My Jesus, forgive our sins, save us from the fires of hell, lead all souls to Heaven, and help especially those in most need of your mercy.

Why have I taught them this prayer? Because I desire the salvation of all the souls, and I wish to teach My children how to ask Jesus for their salvation and for the salvation of their brethren. I want also to reveal to them the existence of hell — to where the souls of sinners who refuse to convert go. However, through prayer, everything can change, since God is attentive to the intercessory prayers for those who are far from the path that leads to Him. I also want to reveal the existence of purgatory to everyone, where the souls suffer and wait for the final moment of their purification, so that they can be eternally united to the Lord in Heaven.

May your hearts be always focused on Heaven and not on the things of this world. Everything will pass away, My children, only God remains. Appertain totally to Jesus, I tell you again. Thank you for your prayers and your presence. I bless all of you: in the name of the Father, of the Son, and the Holy Spirit. Amen!

On July 26, Our Lady emphasizes that "each person in here has a mission to accomplish," and again identifies Itapiranga as a sanctuary which God has especially prepared for young people:

Peace be with you!

Dear children, I am the Queen of Peace and the Mother of Jesus. I am very happy today with your presence and with the presence of My Son's priests.

I call you once more to conversion and prayer. Be with Jesus. Love Jesus. Again I tell you to persevere in your journey towards God, for He never abandons you and is always at your side.

Everyone here has a mission to accomplish. I have not gathered you here for nothing, but to help you to comprehend more and more the mission that God has reserved for you. My little children, I call you to pray more to the Holy Spirit, asking Him for the knowledge and true discernment of your mission.

I have noble things to tell you, and the Almighty invites you to live a holier life, through me.

Each day, more and more, my work of salvation and conversion, entrusted to me by My Son Jesus, is taking place, through my apparitions in the world.

Itapiranga, Itapiranga, sanctuary of grace and blessings that God has prepared for the young people of the whole world and for all families.

Pray for peace in the hearts on My children. Many do not have peace in their lives, because they are far from God. If you pray, abundant love and peace will come down to the world.

I bless all of you: in the name of the Father, of the Son, and the Holy Spirit. Amen!

"*Each word from my messages is like a loving heartbeat from my Immaculate Heart,*" Our Lady tells us (July 28, 2001). She, moreover, encourages us to "*always approach Jesus in the Eucharist*":

Peace be with you!

Dear children, I love you very much and I always wish to lead you to My Son Jesus.

My maternal love pushes Me to come here again, to this place, chosen and blessed by the Lord, to invite you to live a holier life.

Be always united in prayers, as an act of worship and gratitude to the Lord, Who continues to perform His wonders in the world.

My little children, you shall always come closer to Jesus in the Eucharist. Only He is the life for your souls, and your strength during times of trials.

Pray and sacrifice yourselves for those who do not believe in God and do not love Him. Know that your prayers are very precious in the eyes of God. You are helping your brethren, who are far from the path of salvation, to return to it with a contrite heart.

Do not fear anything! Your celestial Mother is always accompanying you with a maternal care. I will help you to be faithful to God if you let yourselves be guided by Me and open up your hearts.

Each word from My messages is like a loving heartbeat from my Immaculate Heart. Every beat of my Heart is a call to a soul. When you are united and praying, you find strength to walk with faith in this faithless world.

Amen, glorify and truthfully worship the Lord of Heaven and earth, and your lives shall be transformed.

It is time for you to deliver ever more My messages to the youth. I send you today to your brothers and sisters, so that you may deliver to them My Maternal plea and love.

Dear young people, thank you for your disposition and contribution to this plan of love from My Lord.

Ask for wisdom from the Omnipotent and He shall grant it to you; so that you will know what to do, how to speak and how to act. Courage. Courage. Now, many are ready to do something for their brethren. This is the moment to show everyone the light of God that shines within you. To all of you, I give my blessing once more: in the name of the Father, the Son, and the Holy Spirit. Amen!

The following message comes directly from Jesus and refers to the "indefatigable" character of Our Lady. Our Lord also relays the truth that the holy names of Jesus, Mary, and Joseph are powerful shields against evil and danger (July 29, 2001):

May My peace be with all of you!

My little children, I'm Jesus, the Son of the Eternal Father and of the Blessed Virgin Mary. I love you all and I wish to have you in My arms. My embrace is strong and I wish to protect you against all evil.

My hands are always extended towards you because I desire to bless you. How glad am I to see your response of love to Me and to My heavenly Mother.

My Mother is the Queen of Peace, because She is united with Me in heaven for all eternity. From Heaven She prays for you, pleading before My throne for the necessary graces for all of you.

My mother is restless. She wishes happiness for all of you. Today She asked me to come to bless you, that is why I am here.

She is the Queen of Heaven and earth, of all Angels and Saints in paradise. In Her humility, meekness, and silence, the great mystery of human salvation has begun, through My coming to this world and, once again, I wish to grant you the grace of salvation through Her Immaculate heart.

Come to My Immaculate Mother, so that holiness will come faster into your lives. Her Most Blessed Name (Mary) is a powerful shield against all evil and danger, just as the Most Holy Name of My father Joseph.

Always invoke these two Most Holy Names, united to My Sacred Name, then graces and blessings from heaven will come down upon you and your family.

I am always with you, by your side, My little ones, and today I place in your little hearts some of My divine love so that you may learn how to love and to serve.

What a deep mystery it is to know how to love and to serve, donating yourself to your neighbor and to the one most in need. When you lay down your life to your brethren, your souls are purified and set free from faults and worldly attachments, and so you are more united to Me and to Heaven.

Wherever your brethren are, there I also am. I always wait for you in your brethren, to grant you My love and My blessings. When you love those who do not love you, you become more and more like me.

Amen, Amen, Amen. Now I bless you with a special blessing. May you be witness of My presence and my appeals to all your brethren. I bless you all In the name of the Father, and of the Son, and of the Holy Spirit. Amen.

In early September, 2001, before the infamous tragedy of September 11, 2001 in New York, Our Lady came to Edson's mother, Maria and asked for immediate prayers, as "many will die." Maria heard screams and cries during the mystical exchange:

Pray, Maria do Carmo (Mary of Carmel), otherwise many will die. Pray, my daughter, help Me with your prayers and pray much for God's mercy for the world.

Edson: My mother heard the voice of several people screaming and crying in distress.

Our Lady then appeared again on September 11th with large tears rolling down her face. Edson recorded his mother's experience of Our Lady on September 11 as follows:

Edson: Our Lady appeared crying. Thick tears rolled down Her face. She did not give any message. She covered Her face with Her hands and cried, disappearing right after. Who can understand the pain She felt in Her heart and the sadness in Her face for what had happened? Let us console Our Holy Mother by changing our lives, and abandoning the path of sin that each day makes other victims.

The following day, September 12, 2001, Edson recorded Our Lady's deep sadness in response to the infamous September 11th event:

Edson: Our Lady is very sad these days. She asks for prayers for the world and for peace. Let us pray to help Her fulfill Her plan of conversion and salvation of humanity. Each prayer is precious and a source of life and grace to the world, and light to the hardened and gloomy hearts.

On November 14, 2001, Our Lady identified herself as, "Our Lady of the Immaculate Conception!" She begged the peoples of the Amazon region for more prayers in order to preserve them from war. She also expressly requested the faithful to spend ten minutes in Eucharistic Adoration after Mass for this intention:

My peace to you and your family, Maria do Carmo. I am Our Lady of the Immaculate Conception!

I come from heaven to beg the people of Amazonas to pray more so that they may be preserved from suffering the consequences of the war. Make a one-hour vigil every day. Remain daily in prayer. Go to adoration to the Holy Sacrament after the Mass, at least ten minutes a day, asking for the end of the war in the whole world. This is the request of a very much afflicted and concerned Mother. Thank you for responding to My call. May My peace and the peace of My Son be with you: In the name of the Father, and of the Son, and of the Holy Spirit. Amen!

Edson: The Holy Virgin left this message to my mother after the terrorist attacks on September 11th. Two days before this attack she had appeared and told her to pray much asking God to be merciful to the world, because something very sad and terrible would strike humanity. The Virgin delivered this message to My mother with a painful heart. For that reason, She asked for prayers on the intention of the end of the war and asking for divine protection because new armed conflicts had begun, which could reach other countries if prayers and reparation were not offered to God.

When the Virgin asked for the ten minutes daily adoration, she meant to show us that many do not devote not even five minutes to the Holy Sacrament. She asked for at least ten minutes because it is good to be in adoration for an extended time. However, many have not yet opened their hearts to this request, living it deeply. When chastisement comes to the world, many will desire to adore Jesus, to beg Him for strength, to be with Him in the Most Holy Sacrament, but they will not be able to, because there might not be enough time left. And God will show them that they could have done that before, in peace and tranquility, but they did not want to, by despising and losing the opportunity and the grace to adore Him in the churches, in the Most Blessed Sacrament.

The Queen of the Rosary and of Peace ends the 2001 year of formidable prophetic messages on the Solemnity of the Holy Family (December 30, 2001) with this succinct request for us to become "Light for the world" and to "pray for good to subdue evil" in family life:

> *Be a light to this world that does not live peace. Pray that goodness subdue evil in your families.*

CHAPTER VI

HEART OF THE MESSAGE
OF ITAPIRANGA

A s mentioned at the beginning of this work, I
originally asked Edson Glauber to select from the
vast quantity of messages he received over 20 years
(literally thousands of individual messages) which heavenly
communications, in the visionary's opinion, constituted the
most central and vital messages revealed by the Hearts of Jesus,
Mary, and Joseph during the historic Itapiranga phenomena.

In other words, what, according to the visionary, constitutes
the *heart of the message of Itapiranga*?

This final chapter is Edson's answer to that question.

This chapter represents a full compendium of Itapiranga
messages from the years 1994, 1995, 1996, 1997, and 2001 as
selected by the visionary—now in the English language for
the first time.

Please keep in mind that the preceding chapters offered a
selection of many of the messages sent to me by Edson (and
grouped by the respective year). *But, this chapter alone contains
all the messages identified by the seer as predominant and central to
the message of the Three Hearts from the Amazonas.*

For this reason, I strongly recommend the prayerful reading of this entire chapter. The message selection that took place in the earlier chapters, for the sake of introduction, thematic accentuation, and brevity, possesses the inherent danger of personal subjectivity in seeking to determine the "best of the best" for the sake of content summation and accentuation. It will therefore do your soul good (as well as mine) not to rely on my personal highlighting of messages, but to take the appropriate time in spiritually and meditatively consuming all the messages which comprise the quintessential heart of Itapiranga.

Our small endeavor here will not end with a dramatic conclusion—and that for two reasons.

First, *the message of Itapiranga continues today*. As of this writing (2017), Edson continues to receive and transmit supernatural messages from the Hearts of Jesus, Mary, and Joseph. There are also efforts underway to have the entire body of as of yet untranslated Portuguese messages of Itapiranga translated into English. I would therefore recommend (rather than any connotation of closure) to encourage you to seek out and read the other inspired messages of the Three Hearts to humanity by going to the official sanctuary website (www.santuariodeitapiranga.com.br) and clicking the setting for English under the "Mensagens" category. Continue to read and be spiritually nourished by these heavenly communications provided to us through the infinite love and generosity of Abba Father for our contemporary salvation and peace.

Secondly, the "drama" of Itapiranga is contained within itself and within its profoundly anointed, inspired, and potentially life changing message. One's heart should leap on its own accord, being prompted and elevated by the Holy Spirit through the Immaculate Heart of Mary—propelling each one of us to an ongoing living of this celestial call.

Itapiranga calls for action. Not just for our own sakes, but for the sake and salvation of our family members, friends, and total strangers we should call brothers and sisters, members of the same human family who, without our personal increase in prayer and sacrifice, run the proximate risk of being eternally lost. As the Mother's Heart has repeatedly wept tears of blood over the loss of her children for all eternity, so should our hearts, and thus prompting us into a new generosity of spiritual and corporal action.

Live Itapiranga. Consecrate yourself daily to the Three Hearts, experience their protection and peace, and pass it on to whomever you sense the Three Hearts inspire you to do so. In a special way, spread devotion to the Most Chaste Heart of St. Joseph. Give joy to the Hearts of Jesus and Mary by loving and daily consecrating yourself, your family, your parish, and anything over whom or which you have spiritual jurisdiction, to His Most Chaste Heart—and then witness and testify to the historic torrents of grace that will result.

In sum, ***Pray*** and ***Prepare***.

CHAPTER VII

THE MESSAGES
OF ITAPIRANGA

1994, 1995, 1996, 1997, 2001

MESSAGES OF 1994

May 11, 1994

Jesus: *Maria do Carmo!*

Maria do Carmo: *I feel so happy. Who is calling me?*

Jesus: *Do not fall asleep!*

Maria do Carmo: *I have to sleep. If I do not, I will feel sleepy tomorrow.*

Jesus: *Get up and write it down. Do not waste time.*

My mother got up, as if a force had pulled her out of bed. She went to the kitchen and looked for a pen and paper to jot it down. She could not find a notebook, but she noticed a loaf of bread on the table wrapped by a sheet of paper. She took the wrapping and used it to write the message from Jesus. When my mother wrote it down, she had not realized that Jesus Himself had inspired her to do so. He wanted to show us and the world that He is the Living Bread that came down from Heaven. He gave the following message:

Jesus to Maria do Carmo:

> *Adultery is a serious sin, but it can be forgiven with a good confession and total repentance. Teach. You know how to make a good confession. Do not be afraid or ashamed of the priest. If the priest forgives, so do I. If he does not forgive, neither do I. Whoever is married and is now separated should again be reconciled if they still love each other—with forgiveness and sincerity!*

> *Whoever is married and is estranged, and is living with another person who is not their spouse should separate and live as friends in the same house. They can no longer live as husband and wife. If one of them is free to marry and have a conjugal life, this person should then get married. One can simply not commit adultery!*

Jesus transmitted this message to my mother because she was concerned about her siblings who were living in adultery, or in common-law marriages and she wanted to know something about it in order to pass on to them and to those who live with them.

May 13, 1994

Our Lady to Edson:

My Army Is Being Built

> *From my heart emanates rays of grace to all of you. Pray hard to console the heart of my Son Jesus.*

This is another important apparition in which the Virgin reveals that the heart of her Son Jesus needs to be consoled, because there is too much sin in the world. She reveals that through Her Immaculate Heart we can receive the grace that will help us to be faithful to Jesus and to comfort Him by doing His Holy Will.

Our Lady to Edson:

My army is being built. One by one, I am knocking at your hearts, opening and preparing them for My Son, Jesus. Open up your hearts now, because my Son is already coming to stay with you!

Today, my mother saw Our Lord in our living room showing a river of crystal-clear water. Jesus was blessing its waters. My mother understood that the river was the grace that Jesus wants to grant to the Amazon and to the world, through the apparitions of Our Lady. This river came from the place where Our Lady appeared for the first time. This place is a source of grace from Heaven. Each place where the Virgin has appeared and appears is a source of grace for all humanity.

Our Lady to Edson:

Four Rosary Mysteries

Turn your television off. Do not watch TV. There is nothing worthy to be seen on television nowadays. Pray constantly. Pray the rosary, for the world needs a great deal of prayer. Pray and do penance. Pray the Rosary every day, preferably on your knees, during one week. You need to do penance for your sins. You need to hear my messages more.

June 22, 1994

In one vision, Our Lady appeared with Her Son Jesus Christ and St. Michael the Archangel at a site in Itapiranga. My mother experienced this vision while being at our home in Manaus. From where she was, in her living room, she saw the

Most Blessed Virgin in Itapiranga with Jesus and St. Michael, at a place which belonged to my father. Jesus and Our Lady were seated and St. Michael was standing at the Virgin's side. My mother explained to me that they seemed to be very near her. This apparition is very important, since it referred to one of the Virgin's requests, which will have great effect in the history of the apparitions: the construction of a chapel in Her honor, the **Queen of Peace.** Here for the first time She shows her desire to be honored with this title.

Our Lady to Edson:

I Have Chosen the City of Itapiranga During the End of Times

I want you to build a provisional little straw chapel at this place. Here in the state of Amazonas, I have chosen the city of Itapiranga for the end of times. In the other locations where other apparitions are occurring and where I have been giving my messages, my apparitions are about to be concluded. And then in Itapiranga, they will begin.

Jesus to Maria:

Obey My Mother

Obey My Mother. Do whatever She asks you to do. Do not remain idle. You have become too much inert. Take action. You have to be humble, caring, kind, loving and obedient. Go visit the imprisoned, the sick at the hospitals, the abandoned children, the neglected elders and widows. Do penances. You know you have to be vigilant.

Another apparition, with a very important message: Here Jesus expressed His wishes for us to do acts of mercy, so that we too may achieve mercy. We cannot remain indifferent to sufferings of our brothers who suffer most. It is Jesus who is asking this of each one of us.

Our Lady appeared to my mother and gave her a very important message regarding what should happen in Itapiranga, clearly expressing what God wished to do in that place:

> *My Son and I have chosen this family, your family, to summon the people to pray more, here in Manaus and in Itapiranga.*
>
> *The city of Itapiranga will be a holy City if all of you pray! What happened in Fatima in 1917 may also happen here. The Enemy wants to reign in this town, but he will not succeed.*

July 15, 1994
To Maria do Carmo:

Pray the Rosary of Love Every Day and All Day Long

> *The woman is the one responsible for everything that happens within her house or her family. She is responsible for the conversion of her children, of her husband, and afterwards, for the conversion of her relatives and close kin. As she was able to win his heart for date and marry her, in like manner she should lead him to daily prayer. Not only for a single day, but for as long as she lives. Don't you feed yourself every day? Likewise, you should also do with prayer.*
>
> *As one who labors has the right to eat, the one who does not labor does not eat either. So it is with salvation. Whoever prays will be saved, but the one who does not, will not be saved. Salvation depends on each person, but the [spiritual] help of a woman, or of a mother or friend is welcomed. I want the conversion of all people, all of them!*

This warning is for every person from the same household or family. Thus, all of them will convert. Announce it. Do not remain inert. Cheer up. Take action. Pray the Rosary of love every day and all day long.

October 15, 1994
Feast of St. Teresa of Avila
Our Lady to Edson:

The Three Hearts

Would you like to sacrifice for the remission of your sins? Love me. Let your love be your penance. My son, write down my message of love for my other children: I am the Mother of God and I come to you because this is my Son Jesus' desire! The Church needs prayers without ceasing. Pray for my children priests; they need your prayers.

Love has to sprout from the bottom of your hearts. Love each other as my Son Jesus loves you. Pray the holy Rosary with love, with your heart. Meditate upon the sacred mysteries of the Rosary. My Son Jesus always waits for you with open arms. He deeply desires to help you overcome every trouble found in your earthly journey. Call on Him, and He shall help you. He is your greatest friend!

I am the Mother of the Church and all of you are my children. Trust and seek refuge in the Sacred Heart of Jesus and in My Immaculate Heart. Love shall reign in your hearts! Write it down [to them]: so that they can believe as if they had seen Me. Do not be burdened by affliction. Peace shall reign in your hearts, the peace that comes from God!

My Children, I cannot answer all your inquiries, for I obey primarily the will of the One who has sent Me, to whom I submit Myself humbly. I cannot interfere in the plans that God has set for each one of you. I can only indicate the means and the way to which each one of you may fulfill the will of the Lord: through prayer, penance, sacrifices, the Word of God, and the Eucharist. Always pray the Rosary and you will have the power to overcome your tribulations. Do not wait for answers because you will not have them. Read the Bible. There you shall find your answers. Nonetheless, I tell you: convert. Change your lives. Follow my instructions and you will receive abundant divine grace.

Prayer shall be for you a reason for joy, of an encounter with God. If you have not achieved this goal, you will hardly ever have peace in your hearts. You need to strive every day to develop a "spirit of prayer." I cannot perform this for you, because the task to improve yourselves each day belongs to you. Only thus shall you be able to decide for God.

Consecrate yourselves every day to our Sacred Hearts, Mine and My Son Jesus', and offer us your preoccupations, jobs, trials and tribulations, for the conversion of souls of the poor sinners. Remain watchful! Pray that you do not fall into temptation, for the Enemy tries at all cost to lead each one of you to his dark and mortal path. Pray without ceasing so that you may overcome him. Guard yourselves with the Rosary and the Word of God. Once more, I beseech you that love may reign in your hearts! With love, you may perform great things and wonders in your lives. My children, live in love! Always keep your hearts open to My Son, Jesus. Jesus is deeply saddened by the lack of love in humanity. For that reason, love, love, love. Let love be your greatest goal. The more you love, the more you will be purified day after day.

My heart and my Son Jesus' are united in love. Likewise, you need to be united in constant love with your heavenly Father and with your neighbor. Live my messages. Listen to my pleas, so that you may experience joy while still on this earth, and later be joyful in the heavenly glory. I love you and I bless all of you in the name of the Father, the Son, and the Holy Spirit. Amen. Praise be to Our Lord Jesus Christ!

October 29, 1994

Our Lady to Edson:

A Great Chastisement is Coming for the Whole World

Pray, pray, and pray. Pray unceasingly! God, Our Lord, is very sad because of your sins. My heart is covered with thorns and pierced by a sword of pain because of your sins. Love each other.

Do not keep hatred and resentment in your hearts. Confess your sins so that you will be free from Satan's hands. The devil is leading many of My children's souls to hell. I need all of you to help me save these souls.

You need to be light for all of these children of Mine. Deny yourselves. Set an example. Do not disregard My Motherly supplications, who suffers for what is about to happen to you. A great chastisement is coming for the whole world, and it is already at hand! Many will suffer if there is no conversion; so, pray the Rosary every day for Brazil and for the peace of the whole world.

October 31, 1994

Monday, dawn:

The Most Blessed Virgin appeared to my mother very sad and crying tears of blood. The Virgin told her:

> *My Son and I are crying tears of blood! There are many souls taking the path to hell. Pray, pray, pray! Pray at the cenacle this ejaculatory prayer that you shall now learn:*

> **Beloved Father, I love Thee. Beloved Mother, I love Thee. Beloved Father and Beloved Mother I love Thee, I love Thee, I love Thee!**

> *… Three times with your heart.*

MESSAGES OF 1995

January 3, 1995

Our Lady to Edson:

Pray That My Plans Will Succeed

> *Visit my Son Jesus in the Blessed Sacrament, because He feels forsaken with no one to visit Him. Confess your sins and ask God for forgiveness for your daily offenses. May My child Jesus bless you and grant you His peace. Pray and fast.*

> *Beloved children, pray that all my plans come true in this city and in the entire world as soon as possible. I am the Immaculate Conception. Satan is furious to see that you are praying, but fear not. I will protect you and keep you all under my mantle.*

January 4, 1995

My children, do penance for sinners, for the salvation of many souls. The world is living in great sin; for that reason, I invite you to pray the Rosary every day for the peace of the world, and for the conversion of sinners. Dearest children, the special message that I bring to you today is this: repent. Open your hearts to God. Pray that all my plans be fulfilled.

January 5, 1995

Pray Continually to Request the Protection of the Archangel St. Michael

Announce my messages and requests to My children; for I want all of them under My mantle. I come with My Son, Jesus, accompanied by St. Michael the Archangel, and with My angels to pray with you and to collect your prayers. Pray continually to request the protection of the Archangel St. Michael, so that he will defend you from the attacks of Satan. I bless all of you in this moment, and I bestow My grace upon each one of you. My Son Jesus is very happy with your prayers. Keep praying.

January 7, 1995

Turn off your television

Beloved children, I ask you: do not waste your time in front of a television; you are giving away precious hours of prayers and dialogue with God. Renounce the television programs. Turn off your television. Offer sacrifices for yourself and for other sinners. Have the practice of reading the Bible. Make an effort to read the Word of My Son, Jesus. Confess your sins more often and go to the Holy Mass. Pray for Brazil. Let the women set the example by their way of dressing. I wish to see again the use of the veil during the celebration of the Holy Mass and in the Church. Let the children pray the Rosary. I bless them and place them always within My heart.

January 8, 1995

I Call Parents to Teach Their Children How to Pray the Rosary as a Family

Dear children, love the Cross of My Son Jesus, who died for love of you on the cross. May every family have a cross of Jesus in their homes. My children, have faith. Pray asking God our Lord to increase your faith; because you need faith to live with love all that I tell you.

Let parents teach their children how to pray the Rosary, praying it united as a family. Everyone who prays the rosary with faith and confidence will receive many blessings from Me and My Son Jesus.

My children, do not slander anyone. May your lips only utter words of joy and comfort to your brethren. Pray for the unity of families. Pray with your hearts. Open your hearts to the Lord. Make My messages known to the other children who are living in sin.

January 10, 1995

The True Church is the Roman Catholic Apostolic Church

Beloved children, there is only One God and one Faith. Do not be deceived by the snares and false religions instituted by Satan. The true Church founded by My Son, Jesus Christ, which is worthy of faith, is the Roman Catholic Apostolic Church, which has in the holy Father the representative of My Son Jesus ...Obey the Church and follow its teachings with living faith and you shall be saved.

January 13, 1995

Carry the Rosary with You Wherever You Go

Pray the Rosary every day. May every family pray the Rosary and each one of my children carry his own. This weapon defends them from the Evil One. Use it daily. Carry it with you wherever you go. Pray the Rosary, dear children. Listen to My petitions. I bless all of you with the blessings of joy, so that you will pray to the Lord with great fervor.

January 15, 1995

Don't Wound My Immaculate Heart with Your Doubts

Dear children, I am your Mother; hence, don't harm my Immaculate Heart with your doubts. Pray with your hearts, little children. Help me, dear children; do penance for sinners, because many souls are at risk of eternal damnation, since they have no one to pray and make sacrifices for them. Pray the holy Rosary every day for your brethren who find themselves in the path of sin, and for yourselves.

Little children, I beseech you: listen and live what I am asking from each of you, otherwise many souls may be cast down into hell. My children, I still see many sins within you; thus confess your sins. Cleanse your souls, little children. Go to Holy Mass with a purified heart. Prepare yourselves in advance with prayers and contrite souls so that you be prepared to receive my Son, Jesus, who is in the Holy Eucharist.

Little children, abandon the vices of this world. Renounce in particular, smoking, alcohol, and television programs. Know that it is Jesus who is requesting this. And I, as His humble servant, deliver to you His message. May the mothers instruct their children to pray the holy Rosary and that each family pray it united. I leave you an urgent and worrying message: convert yourselves as soon as possible. You do not know what God will send to the world if there is no conversion.

January 20, 1995

Don't Be My Incredulous Children

Don't be incredulous, my little children. Open your eyes and see how the world is today. Should I, as your Mother, not be concerned to the point of coming to warn you of the dangers if there is no conversion? My message is very serious, and I have come every day to call you to convert, to repent and return to the Lord. Little children, return to the Lord. Do not remain in sin. Fight against Satan. Overcome Him with frequent recitation of the holy Rosary. I am always with you although you do not see me. Thank you for your prayers. Today your prayers are assisting a multitude of souls. Pray even more.

January 21, 1995

Let Your Consecration Be Genuine and Open Your Hearts

Pray intensively for the unity of families. Satan, during these troubled times you live in, attacks many families leading to quarrels, misunderstanding, and many divorces. Pray in order that his plans might be destroyed.

My beloved children, I have great love for you. The Lord wishes that each one of you be closer to My Immaculate Heart, so that I may keep you and protect you from Satan's attacks. Little children, consecrate yourselves to My Immaculate Heart and to the Sacred Heart of My Son Jesus. May your consecration be genuine, open your hearts to Me. Seek refuge in My Immaculate Heart. Always recite the consecration that My children have taught you. I promise to intercede with my Son, Jesus, for the salvation of the ones who consecrate themselves to me. Approach the Eucharist, My children. Read the Holy Bible and make sacrifices for the sinners. Ask My Son supplicating for your conversion and pray with Me. Let us unite our prayers to save the souls of sinners. Praying with you brings Me great joy. I always join you in prayer when I am invited to participate. I am the Queen of Peace, the Mother of God, the Mother of sinners and your Mother.

January 23, 1995

Jesus Waits in the Eucharist
With an Immeasurable Love

Renounce Satan by praying the Rosary and attending Mass in order to belong entirely to Jesus. Jesus waits for you in the Eucharist with an immeasurable love. Come to the Holy Mass to belong to Him totally. Confess your sins. Do not receive My Son, Jesus, if you are in grave sin. First cleanse yourselves through holy confession. There is a risk of eternal damnation for many, when they live indifferently in sin without seeking confession as they should. Be sincere with My Son Jesus Christ, who poured out all of His Blood and gave His Life for your salvation.

January 28, 1995
Afternoon:

Little children, read the Holy Bible, pray the Rosary and confess your sins. Do not live in a sinful state; your sins separate you from the grace of God. Pray for yourselves. Love your own selves; for whoever loves, loves his own beautiful life, and learn how to love his neighbor.

Evening:

Little children, let us come together with Jesus, who waits for us with open arms. Offer Him your lives, your work, and your daily tribulations. Be strong. Be prepared every day and at every moment with cleansed souls, free from the blemish of sin. Confess your sins when in need! Do not live without confession, for God wishes to find you cleansed and pure every day. Little ones, pray and do penance for poor sinners, since many souls may be eternally lost to hell due to the lack of sacrifices and prayers for them. Pray, pray more!

February 14, 1995
St. Michael the Archangel:

A Torrent of Chastisements

Today I come to bring a very important message directly from the Most Blessed Virgin Mary, Mother of God. Do penance and make sacrifices to redeem the souls of poor sinners. Push yourselves to pray the Rosary and pray it especially for peace in the entire world, because the world is urgently in need of it.

The most Holy Virgin has come to the world on many occasions during these recent times to call you to repentance and to return to the Lord. However, She has not been heard as She should because of men's ingratitude. Do not reject the messages that the Mother of God herself has been conveying to you for a while now. Pay heed to them and act upon them as soon as possible; for the present times are very urgent and concerning.

The World has completely forsaken the Lord and despises Him every moment. How much suffering has been inflicted to the most Holy Virgin. She sheds tears of blood, supplicating the Father's mercy to this perverse and sinful world. She asks the Father to pour His peace and His love upon humanity, so that punishment might be avoided.

You do not know what may be coming for this unfortunate sinful humanity. Pray, asking My powerful protection and I promise to pray to the Lord for each one of you. Pray asking peace for the world. Visit the most Holy Sacrament of the altar, devoting hours of reparation to Our Lord, who so intensely suffers due to blasphemies, ingratitude, and disrespect coming from mankind at each moment. Pray, children of the Lord, pray.

February 14, 1995
Our Lady to Edson:

The World Needs Many Prayers and Sacrifices

The world needs lots of prayers and sacrifices! Our Lord is about to send a torrent of chastisements and I do not know what else I can do to prevent it. Pray, pray my beloved children! Do not offend God, Our Lord, any longer. He already feels so offended. Supplicate God for forgiveness for your offenses and He will forgive you. My Immaculate Heart suffers because only a few pay heed to my messages. How much this hurts My heart! My children are so ungrateful to Me and to My Son Jesus! Pray for the end of this ingratitude. Do not offend the Lord, for you have hurt Him enough. Here I am, as Mother of Grace and Mercy, to help you walk on the long road until you reach the Lord.

I am the Queen of Peace, your Mother and Mother of God. Pray the Rosary every day so that the world will definitely find the peace it so desperately needs. Visit Jesus in the Most Holy Sacrament of the altar more frequently. Do not forsake so many graces. Strive to receive these graces profusely, through prayers to Jesus in the Blessed Sacrament.

February 15, 1995
St. Michael the Archangel:

The Tears Shed by the Blessed Virgin Are Postponing the Punishment

Son of the Lord, here is My message for today, sent directly from the Lord and from the Most Holy Virgin. You must make sacrifices and penances for the conversion of poor sinners. Visit the Blessed Sacrament of the altar frequently to make reparation to Jesus in the Eucharist. He is enduring constant transgressions from sinners, especially now that, in your country, carnival holiday is approaching. Therefore, I, St. Michael, as commanded by God, invite you to pray for amendment, committing every deed done throughout from day to day, in atonement and penitence for the conversion of the ungrateful sinners. Everything is worth doing when it is done and delivered with love to our God and our Lord Jesus Christ. The Most Holy Virgin insistently asks her beloved children to publicly worship Her Son in the Blessed Sacrament, to keep vigils and do acts of reparation to the Lord, and ask Jesus Christ to pour the grace from His Mercy over all of you, here in this city, in the state of Amazonas, and especially in Brazil and the entire world, so that His plans be fulfilled as soon as possible.

Pray the Rosary every day, especially the ones from the tears of blood from the Blessed Virgin Mary; the tears poured out by the Holy Virgin are postponing the punishment that might come against humanity.

Jesus refuses nothing because of the tears of His Most Blessed Mother. The Blessed Virgin has daily offered the merits of Her Son Jesus Christ to the Father, along with Her tears of blood, so that abundant blessings and graces of conversion may be bestowed upon the world, especially to those most hardened by sin. The current times are urgent and very critical; still, you have paid little attention to the ones chosen by the Holy Virgin to spread these messages. Return children of God, return. The Father will not hesitate to deliver His Divine anger over the ones who have rejected Him. Those who reject Him will remain with Satan and his followers. I, St. Michael, the Archangel, along with St. Gabriel and St. Raphael, and all the angels, bless you: in the name of the Father, the Son and the Holy Spirit. Amen.

The Most Blessed Virgin appeared during the evening. She was weeping tears of blood. Large tears were falling from her beautiful blue eyes.

February 15, 1995
Our Lady to Edson:

What have you done since yesterday to diffuse my messages? I need your help. Pray the Holy Rosary. Don't remain idle. Take action!

February 16, 1995

Sacrifice and offer to my Son, Jesus, all that is most dear to you, in reparation for the offenses practiced by ungrateful sinners. Flee from every impurity my children! I especially request that you do not watch television during these days, because it only spreads sinful and impure images. Primarily now that carnival is approaching. Flee from carnival as if you were fleeing from the hands of the Devil, for carnival is the feast of the Devil himself. Go to Church to pray during this period to offer reparations to Jesus for your sins and for the sins of your brethren.

February 18, 1995

Pray the Rosary and You Shall Subdue Satan

Little children, the world needs immediate conversion! Many of you do not want to acknowledge the Lord, and despise Him all the time. Satan takes many of my children's souls to hell at every moment. This brings me great pain, My children! What would be a mother's reaction to see her little child burning in a large fire, being unable to do anything? Think about it My children, for such is My sorrow when I see my children rushing into the fire of hell. Many refuse to believe in hell, but I tell you, little ones, it does exist and it is terrifying! Many who have refused all the messages I conveyed these past years are now in hell because they ignored my messages and wasted many blessings from My Immaculate Heart.

Oh Dear children, pray, pray and pray. Do not despise anything that I tell you, but convert! I am your Mother and I love you so much. Ask me for help and I shall help you immediately. I wish that you pray the Rosary every day; for the Rosary is the weapon which I offer you during these last days to fight against the Devil who is

endlessly persecuting you! Pray the Rosary and you shall
overcome Satan.

February 19, 1995

In the morning, I was praying at the hill, by the cross at the apparition site, from where we can see the tower of Our Lady of Nazareth church. Our Lady appeared and told me:

I have truly appeared in Ghiaie di Bonate!

She then blessed me and disappeared. I returned home thinking about that name: Bonate, Bonate! I did not know how to pronounce it well. When I got home, I told my mother: today Our Lady appeared at the hill while I was praying and she uttered a strange name: Bonate! My mother asked me: What is Bonate? I answered: it was a place where She appeared but people didn't believe, otherwise she wouldn't have told me that she indeed had appeared there.

February 21, 1995

Don't be skeptical my children. Listen to Me: time is very
short and many do not pay heed to the Maternal messages
that I convey today as well as the other messages which I
have announced the world over. Pray the Rosary every
day for the salvation of the poor sinners. Listen to Me
little children. Do as I say, otherwise a great chastisement
will soon befall upon the whole world because of the
innumerable sins that are committed by mankind at
every moment…

Our Lady cried deeply. Tears streamed down from her beautiful blue eyes. How heartbreaking it is to see the Virgin crying! One wants to console and comfort her immediately so that She no longer suffers for us.

> *...How much I suffer to see My children falling into hell! May parents love their children as my Son Jesus loves them. May mothers love their children as I love them and as I love my Son Jesus, because they are their greatest treasures, more precious than jewels. There is no greater wealth in the world that can be compared to the children God has granted them. Fathers and mothers I ask of you: love your children; for one day, God our Lord will ask an account for each child He has given you. How heartbreaking it is to see mothers killing their own children inside their wombs. How I suffer for that! Little children, help Me with your prayers to save those souls. Pray for the end of abortion. Dry the tears flowing down from the face of your Heavenly Mother, as a result of all that I see today.*

After Our Lady gave me that message, the sky became cloudy, since it was about to rain. Nature assumed a sad aspect because Our Lady was crying. Soon, a strong bolt of lightning appeared, followed by an unsettling thunder that shook our house. The Virgin said:

> *Soon God, Our Lord, will send a sign meaning that He will punish mankind of its sins and crimes. A thunder much stronger than this which will shake the four corners of the Earth, announcing that the day of the great purification is at hand.*

St. Michael the Archangel appeared afterwards and he told me:

> *God, Our Lord, is not happy with this poor sinful humanity. Pray, Pray, Pray!*

Jesus to Maria:

> *Everyone who has mocked, abused and despised My Holy Mother's messages I say: when I come to this world as the*

Just Judge, each and every one of these people who does not repent from these acts shall be thrown into the fire of hell, as dry wood.

February 22, 1995

Our Lady to Edson:

Queen of the Youth

I am the Queen of the youth, the Mother of God, and here from Itapiranga, I make a call to all young people, as I have never made before: return to My Son Jesus. He loves you. Itapiranga is and shall ever be a call for deep conversion of the young people. I am your Heavenly Mother and I do not want any of you to be lost forever on the road to hell. For this reason I come to your aid, to teach you and show you the path of Salvation, the road that leads to God.

February 25, 1995

Why do you refuse to listen to what I tell you? I am the Mother of God, Pure and Immaculate, conceived since my Immaculate Conception without sin; I tell you: I do not live without God. God is everything to Me. My Son Jesus is My life and My everything.

My children, you who are sinners and fall easily into sin, [you] suppose that you can totally live without God who is your everything. No, my children! No one can live without God. Those who are far from My Son Jesus Christ, who is their God, be assured that they are walking towards eternal damnation.

March 1, 1995

Pray the Rosary and You Will Be Able to Solve All of Your Problems

Little children, I desire to have all of you under my mantle. Pray little ones, pray. Pray especially the blessed Rosary and consecrate yourselves every day to my Immaculate Heart and to the Sacred Heart of My Son Jesus; then you shall see abundant graces from Me and My Son Jesus. Pray the rosary and you will be able to solve all your problems.

Little children, I need your help. See how Satan is operating in the world, causing dissentions, disagreement and lack of comprehension amongst yourselves. I need your prayers, little ones, in order to push Satan away from your lives and your families. Do not worry for I am by your side to help you. I love you so, little ones. My Son Jesus and I are working in the world with only one purpose: the salvation of souls. Listen and live out these appeals of ours that resound all over the world. Do not allow Satan to separate you from My Son Jesus Christ. Pray, pray, pray and you shall overcome the Enemy.

March 2, 1995

Pray The Holy Rosary so That You may Bear Your Daily Struggles

Pray the holy Rosary so that you may bear your daily struggles. Offer your sufferings to Jesus in reparation and expiation for the sins currently committed in the world. Do not be afraid of your cross, dear children. Carry it with joy. Do not give up. Jesus is always by your side to help you carry your cross. He hopes for a little of your love to help save many souls. Without your help, they would be inevitably lost. I am the Lady of the Holy Rosary, Mother of God and your Mother.

March 16, 1995
St. Michael the Archangel:

Pray to Our Beloved Heavenly Queen and You Shall Not Regret It

I am the Archangel St. Michael, I have come to protect you against all assaults, and pour my blessings upon those who heed and carry on the messages of Our Blessed Virgin Mary.

Pray, little children of the Lord, pray the holy Rosary every day. The Lord will reward those who have respectfully and devotedly welcomed His Holy Mother, who is the Queen of the World, Queen of all Saints and Angels. Pray to Our Beloved Heavenly Queen and you shall not regret it.

March 16, 1995
Our Lady to Edson:

Pray and Ask for the Gifts of the Holy Spirit

Pray intensely to the Divine Holy Spirit. Do not abandon the One who is your Light, your true Wisdom and your Life. Pray and ask the gifts of the Holy Spirit for yourselves and for your brethren. If you knew what the Holy Spirit has intended for each one of you, you would pray to Him more so that He would change your lives. The Holy Spirit is entirely love and tenderness. May the Holy Spirit descend upon each one of you and give you His peace, strength, and comfort. May He overshadow you and pour Himself out unto you in grace and abundance. Pray little ones, pray. I am the Virgin of Grace. Pray and I will ask and obtain from the Lord many blessings for each one of you.

Jesus to Edson:

I expect a little aid and love from you. Will you, by the way, respond to My request? Will you listen to my appeal? O little children, how I pity this poor sinful humankind! How deaf are you humans to My heavenly requests! Don't fall asleep, don't stop. Pray, pray, pray. Don't you know that you are witnessing the great times preceding My return to your midst? Be prepared because the time is imminent. For that reason, I have sent you many signs, and the most beautiful one is my Heavenly Mother, who is instructing you to live in My paths and teachings. Listen to Her. Whoever listens to My Mother, listens to Me. Whoever obeys My Mother, obeys Me. The world is deaf and does not listen. Why? Why do they reject and close their eyes and ears to what we ask? Are you weary, my children? Don't you know the time is very urgent? Pray and be on guard so that you do not fall into temptation. I, the Lord, bless you all.

March 20, 1995
Our Lady to Edson:

Do Not Offend Our Lord Anymore, For He Is Already Much Affronted

Here in Itapiranga, to the whole world I make a vehement request: do not offend God, Our Lord, anymore, for He is already much offended! Flee from any and every impurity. Satan leads many souls to hell because of the weakness of humankind sins of the flesh! How sorrowful it is to my Immaculate Heart to see My little ones going to hell! Pray dear young; pray, because it is mostly the souls of the youth that I see being eternally lost in the fire of hell!

March 21, 1995

Our Lady to Edson:

I was praying at the site of the apparitions, in front of the tree where the Virgin usually appeared, and like the other times, She arrived and with a majestic voice and said:

Peace, peace, peace! Humanity ought to pray asking God for peace!

The Blessed Virgin moved through the air and went to the place where she desires the chapel to be built. She asked me to kiss that ground three times in gratitude for the Triune God, for this granted blessing. Then pointing with her finger, she added:

Take this twig and use it to mark the place where I want the chapel be built, which must be here.

I did as she asked me to. The Virgin went ahead indicating with her hand where I was to mark the place with the twig. After everything had been done, the Virgin told those who were witnessing this apparition.

Here in this place I want that a small chapel be built in My honor. May the people hurry up and fulfill the request of Mine. This request comes directly from My Son, Jesus. Let everything that I have conveyed to you recently, through My heavenly warnings and Maternal messages, be fulfilled. Pray the Holy Rosary. Pray, pray, pray. Pray for the peace of the entire world and for the conversion of sinners. Pray for the pope, for the bishops, the priests, and for every consecrated soul. I am the Queen of the World, Queen of Peace, the Mystical Rose. I bless all of you: in the name of the Father, of the Son, and of the Holy Spirit. Amen.

March 23, 1995

Children, pray the holy Rosary. Each Hail Mary is a hard blow against Satan. May the priests pray the Rosary. Many do not pray it. Why not? I need your help. Help your celestial Mother, My little children. Pay heed to my supplications. Live my plea. If you don't listen to my petition you will suffer greatly, because to whom much is given, much is required.

March 24, 1995

Children, I have come here today to invite you to conversion. Our Lord Jesus Christ sent me to Itapiranga to bring you a compelling and serious message: convert immediately! A great evil is about to come over this poor sinful humanity. Get your Rosaries and recite them with great devotion, offering them to my Son Jesus as reparation for the sins of world.

March 25, 1995

St. John the Baptist to Maria:

I am St. John the Baptist. Jesus has sent me here. You shall understand what I came to do.

"Is this about Baptism?" My mother asked.

Yes. That was my mission on earth, and now it applies to the priests. Jesus wants everyone to be baptized. There are many who have not yet been baptized: young women and men. There is no need for so much pomp and formalities to baptize. One must be dressed decently. Any baptized person can be a godparent. Except Freemasons, unless they abandon the Freemasonry. God is inside every person in baptism, through the Holy Spirit.

April 23, 1995

Jesus to Edson in Manaus:

Entrust to My Mercy Your Brethren and the Whole World

I was in Manaus. I was returning home and felt very tired. When I got home, my siblings were not home and I had no key to open the gate and the house door. I was a bit disappointed to have to wait for them outside of the house. At that moment, I heard Jesus' voice:

> *You see, the doors of your house are closed to you but the doors of My House shall never be closed to you or to your relatives, nor to your friends and neighbors, neither to the entire world.*

Later, when I was praying the chaplet of the Divine Mercy around 9:00 PM, the Lord told me:

> *Write down everything that you have heard and felt. My heart is full and rich in mercy. Devote yourself as well as your entire family to my Merciful Heart. Entrust to My Mercy your brethren and the whole world. I wish that the messages given by My Mother in Itapiranga be announced and known.*

Jesus to Maria do Carmo:

> *My sheep know my voice.*

May 5, 1995

Our Lady to Edson:

> *Love each other. Love my Son Jesus. Jesus is Love. Once you start to love your brothers and sisters, then you will learn to recognize Jesus in your lives. Dear children, I invite you to love. Open your hearts to love.*

May 11, 1995

Jesus to Edson:

To Open Your Hearts, You Need a Good and Holy Confession

Love: Love each other as I love you. Open up your hearts. Learn to listen to Me when I speak to your heart. To open up your hearts you need a good and holy confession. Do not accumulate sins in your hearts. Go to confession.

On that day, I was praying with a youth group in a house in Itapiranga. One of the young people asked during the apparition (he was asking to himself): "How can I open my heart? How does one open his heart?" For that reason Jesus answered in that message: *"To open up your hearts you need a good and holy confession. Do not accumulate sins in your hearts. Go to confession."*

June 23, 1995

This work is Mine and I Am the One who opens the doors and roads in front of you. I will take the necessary steps and provide people to help you spread the word about my wishes and the requests of my Mother to the whole world. Pray and have trust.

June 24, 1995

Our Lady to Edson:

Put My Requests Into Action

Dear little children, I am your Mother from Heaven. I, your heavenly Mother, come in this great evening to pour out immeasurable graces from My Immaculate Heart upon each one of you. I beseech you: put my requests into action. Do not leave for tomorrow what you can do today. Make the children pray the Rosary, for we are living times of great conflicts and danger. Pray more, pray more, and more.

July 17, 1995

St. Gabriel the Archangel:

Repair the Offenses Created Against the Sacred Heart of Jesus and the Immaculate Heart of Mary

Son of the Lord, pray, pray, and pray. Make reparations to the offenses against The Sacred Heart of Jesus and the Immaculate Heart of Mary. The hearts of Jesus and Mary are very sorrowful because of the sins committed around the whole world. Comfort Jesus through reparation for the countless sins perpetrated against His Blessed Mother and He Himself. The holy Hearts of Our Lord Jesus Christ and our Most Blessed Virgin Mary are bleeding because of the many sins, sacrileges and blasphemies piercing them as penetrating and prickly thorns. Pray the Rosary and offer it in reparation to Jesus and Mary for the crimes and sins of the whole world. The world is about to face great calamities and dangers, and if reparations, sacrifices and prayers are not offered, it may fall into the large abyss which it has reached. I, the Archangel St. Gabriel, invite you to honor the Most Blessed Virgin Mary, Mother of God, by praying the Rosary, asking Her powerful intercession and protection, since only She can come to your aid in the presence of God Our Lord. Pray, pray, pray!

August 5, 1995

Our Lady to Edson:

Announce my Messages to All of my Children

Make my messages known to all of my children. Come in larger numbers. Here in this place lies the source of grace that I have prepared for each one of you. Everyone who comes to pray with love and devotion shall obtain abundant graces from my Immaculate Heart. I am the Queen of Peace. Pray, pray, pray.

August 22, 1995

God Wishes to Perform Great Things in the Amazon

God wishes to perform great things in the Amazon. I count on your prayers to fulfill everything according to my plans. Pray, pray, pray.

August 29, 1995

Everyone who prays will be sheltered under my mantle in the day of the chastisement.

September 6, 1995

Our Lady to Edson:

Everything is possible for the one who believes!

Jesus to Edson:

Our Lord, fondly looking at me told me:

Take my seeds (the messages) everywhere. Do not be discouraged. Pray, pray.

September 19, 1995
Our Lady to Edson:

Dear Young People, I Desire to Guide You to Complete Sanctity

Dear young people, I desire to guide you to complete sanctity with God, but first you need to pray constantly and take the path of conversion, sacrifice and penance. I need your help. Help me. Beloved youth, change your lives. Renounce the pleasures of this world. Be pure. Convert yourselves. Satan wants to conquer many young people through persuasion and temptations, but you can overcome him by reciting the Rosary. Convert yourselves now! Do not put leave your conversion for tomorrow. I bless everyone who is present here and place you inside my Immaculate Heart. Get together more often to pray. Pray more. Read the Bible, the word of My Son Jesus.

October 12, 1995

I am Black but Beautiful, O ye Daughters of Jerusalem

On a different day, Our Lady gave me a biblical reading. This reading was meant to answer a question of a friend of mine, who was doubtful about Our Lady of Aparecida, because she is black. My friend asked me:

"Edson, is it alright to honor Our Lady of Aparecida as black? Is this in the Bible?"

I answered her: "Look... If God wanted us to honor His Mother as black woman and Our Lady of Aparecida, then this must be based on the Bible, because everything God does is always in the Bible. When I hear something about it, I will let you know!"

Our Lady appeared later that day and said:

Open the Bible and read the Canticle of Canticles 1:5-6.

"I am black but beautiful, Oh ye daughters of Jerusalem, as the tents of Cedar, as the curtains of Solomon. Do not consider me that I am brown, because the sun hath altered my color" (Cant 1:5-6).

November 10, 1995

The Father is Loving to All His Children

God is your Father and your Creator. Thank Him for the great gift of your lives granted by Him. Life is a very special gift, granted by God to every creature. The Father is loving to all of His children, but only few of them are loving towards the Celestial Father. Love God with all your heart and offer Him all your troubles.

November 11, 1995

Many of My Priest-Sons Need Your Prayers

My little ones, do not be unbelieving, but be steadfast in your prayers. Jesus is your peace. Love Jesus and comfort His Heart, which is wounded with love for you. Do not get discouraged my little ones. Take courage. Proceed to the Father's home confidently. Pray for the priests, for the bishops and for the souls who are consecrated to God. Pray, pray for the Holy Church. The Church needs numerous prayers and sacrifices. Many favorite sons are in great need of your prayers to remain firm to the vocation they have been called. They count on your prayers and sacrifice. Pray little ones, pray, pray. The world needs a great deal of prayers and sacrifices. Satan works intensely in this world, trying to destroy every child of the Lord. Satan wants to destroy your lives, my children; thus come to my arms, so that I can protect you from his attacks and traps. I am your Celestial Mother and I am here to defend you from all evil. Free yourselves from sin and confess; then you will be able to take the path that leads to salvation, which is Jesus.

November 12, 1995
Jesus to Edson for priests and bishops:

Do Not Be Impatient and Don't Lose Your Hope

I have come to pour my light and my peace over the Amazon. I wish to help my favorite sons in their arduous task of evangelization. I know how much they have worked to take my Word to every nation and how hard their apostolic work is. For that reason, I tell them: do not be impatient and do not lose hope. I am at your side to help you. My Mother and I are here with open arms to welcome everyone into our Sacred Hearts. My mother and I love you and always look after you on your tribulations, even on the slightest ones. Do not lose heart. Take courage. Live in the peace of My Blessed Heart and in the peace of the Immaculate Heart of My Mother. Spread my image and My peace to the youth. Let the youth see in you My face. Be the reflection of My image. You have received a great mission, the mission of being messengers of God's peace and God's Living Word. Pray more as real apostles of My Church. Be strong in your vocation. Be united to your bishop and help him with your prayers and with your filial love. Do not abandon him, but obey him as obedient children obey their father. I would be very happy if you lived as a true Christian family, united by Christian foundations. There should not be division but only unity among you. I, the Lord Jesus Christ, bless My favorite children, and especially all the bishops along with my dearest among them, the pope.

November 20, 1995

St. Gabriel the Archangel:

Always Pray to St. Joseph

Pray always to St. Joseph. He always defends and protects you against the attacks of Satan. St. Joseph is a great saint before God, who obtains everything through his intercession to the Holy Trinity. The Holy Trinity has granted Him abundant graces so that He might perform his role as protector of the Child God in this world. And today St. Joseph is in the glory of Heaven, with the Holy Trinity, praying for each one of you, for your eternal salvation and in order that you may have full comprehension of the requests of your Celestial Mother.

November 28, 1995

St. Gabriel the Archangel:

Amazonas was Chosen by God to Receive a Great Grace

Amazonas has been chosen by God to receive a great grace. Thank Jesus for everything He is accomplishing here by sending His Most Blessed Mother to your midst. Pray, pray more. Give your heart to Jesus and Mary.

December 13, 1995

Our Lady to Edson:

The Great Purification Will Happen Soon

The cup of Divine Justine is full and overflowing. Soon, great events will destabilize all humanity, renewing all mankind. The great purification will soon take place. Cleanse yourselves now from your sins; free yourselves through holy confession, so that you can endure the day of the coming of the Lord. To the mothers who do not want the children in their wombs to be born and desire to kill them (I say): Repent, repent! For God's anger will fall upon those mothers and fathers who are murderers. Pray to the end of abortion. Pray to the end of violence. Pray much for those who do not believe in God. Do penances for the poor sinners.

My little children, wipe away the tears from your Mother's face, caused by the innumerable sins committed in the world. Many people offend the Lord. Many blaspheme against His Holy name. Make reparation for these terrible sins. Help me, little children. Your celestial Mother awaits for your help. Pray for Brazil. Again, I say to you: if the Brazilian people do not heed my requests, a great punishment will come upon your nation. Pray for it. Jesus loves your nation so much. Pray for it. He has a special grace to accomplish here in Brazil.

December 25, 1995
St. Michael the Archangel:

Our Lady has Her Mantle Over Your Families

Our Lady has her mantle placed upon your families. Jesus and Mary wish to live in your hearts and in your families. They desire to teach you to take the path of sanctity in the families. Thus, your family has been chosen to be an example to the others. This way, they wish to show other families how much they love them. Jesus and Mary wish that all families open their doors to receive them. The Virgin Mary teaches, exhorts and invites you. She wants to guide you but you still do not listen to Her words. It is very important that you be obedient.

Our Lord, the King of all families, wishes to be with you. Know that He Loves you and it was Him who has sent me. Do you understand what I tell you? It is God who has sent me to you. He is the Almighty, Creator of Heaven and Earth, the God of Abraham, God of Isaac, and God of Jacob, according to the Scriptures. He is everything, the Lord of the universe. You have not yet understood it? It is necessary that you open your hearts more. Say to the Lord always: **Lord, open my heart so that I will be able to understand your word as Our Lady does. Amen!**

December 30, 1995

Jesus to Edson:

While I was reciting my prayers, before the Holy Mass in Itapiranga, I heard the voice of Jesus who said:

Satan Will Not be Able to Destroy Your Plans

Fight my son, so that Satan does end up destroying my plans.

I was always being attacked by the Devil. It seemed as if the entire hell had been unleashed against me. I was going through terrible sufferings and strong temptations. I knew that everything was for the work of the Virgin and for the salvation of many young people. How much suffering we need to undergo for the salvation of one soul! Who could imagine what happens within my soul? I am in deep darkness seeking the light of God, but it seems that the Lord's luminous and merciful face is far away for a moment.

Give me the strength, Oh Lord, to endure everything with love and patience, without ever losing faith, hope and trust in You. Let me never act without charity towards my neighbor!

MESSAGES OF 1996

January 13, 1996
The Catholic Church...There is No Other

People are mistaken when they think that My Son and I only appear to the saints, or to those who are sinless. All of you are sinners, because you were conceived in sin. Only my Son and I were born without sin. Remember St. Paul: Paul persecuted the Christians, by attacking my Son's Church, until that day My Son appeared to him and converted him altogether.

It was only then when he started to live a life of sanctity. He was not a saint yet, but fought for this goal until the end of his life. His sermons converted many of my children to My Son Jesus. He is one of the greatest Saints and my loved child. This is how it will be once you start to heed my messages and put into practice the Gospel of My Son Jesus, loving and respecting His Holy Church, which is the Catholic Church, and no other.

January 21, 1996
Our Lady to Maria:

Have faith. Have confidence. Now you have to fast: fast! You have stopped fasting. You have to fast always and do acts of charity. You have to pray, doing penance even inside your home: praying, kneeling down and kissing the ground.

January 24, 1996

Pray Very Much

During the morning, very early, my mother was thoughtful about what God and the Virgin wanted from us, from my family. She was thinking about the reason why God had chosen our family. Suddenly she heard the voice of the Mother of God saying the following message:

> *You ask me what 'we want from you?' We only request that you pray much, very much. Always pray together. Repent from your sins and fast. That is all I wish. This is all that My Son and I desire. We are very close to each other. We are all united. Have you not realized it yet? You already belong to my family… Leave your addictions behind. When you feel the urge to smoke, think about God and pray the Creed. When you pray say always: I am praying to alleviate the sorrows of the heart of my Jesus and the heart of the Virgin Mary. Do not worry about worldly things. Stay with my Jesus!*

January 31, 1996

> *My Son is very sad, little children, with everything that is currently happening in the world. There are lots of errors, errors upon terrible errors, my children. The world is approaching the end: prepare yourselves with abundant prayers, praying for those who still do not see anything, even though their eyes are wide open, my children. I am the Queen of Peace, asking for peace for everyone, every day. Pray, pray very much. Do not be weary in praying for all people. See you soon my daughter!*

I am Crying, My Daughter

Our Lady started to cry, what made my mom very sad, and she also started to cry.

I am crying, my daughter, because of all the bad things that are taking place: serious, grave, horrible sins. See you soon!

March 23, 1996

…Confess the Sin of Sloth

Around 10:00 PM, before going to bed, my mother heard the Virgin voicing a message to her:

Tell the people to confess the sin of sloth when going to confession. Pray to the Holy Spirit and everything will be all right.

March 30, 1996

I am the Mother of All Peoples, Mother of All Humanity

It is necessary for you to pray together. It is necessary to exercise love amidst the families. Families are being destroyed because they lack love and because they do not practice love among themselves. A family that does not exercise love cannot receive My Divine Son, because Jesus is love and He wishes to be in the midst of the families to transmit His love. However the families reject Him because they worry only about their own interests, and their concerns prevent them from feeling Jesus in their hearts. Dear children, you are family. You are my family. I am your Mother, and God is your Father. God desires to see all the families living in a loving communion with Jesus and with their brothers and sisters. My dear children, love each other. Love each other as Jesus loves you and as I love you. As I have said: God will collect every good deed from the heart of men, performed during their journey on earth, after their existence here on earth.

Peace, peace, peace: I proclaim once more! I desire peace among all Christians of the entire world. Christians or not, they all are my children. As My Son Jesus has said, there are still many sheep that have not yet been guided to the same flock, and that do not belong to the same sheepfold. Pray for the union of all Christians.

I am the Mother of all peoples, Mother of all humanity.

When the Holy Spirit sets aflame all hearts with the fire of his love, then all mankind will burn with a holy desire of craving for God above all else, and worldly things will have no room in their hearts because only God will be their unique and genuine treasure. Pray, pray, pray asking the Divine Holy Spirit to pour upon you His light, so that all of you are renewed by His sanctifying grace.

April 8, 1996

Jesus Loves the Young People

Jesus loves the young people: of all the apostles, John was the youngest one, and the one much loved by my Son Jesus Christ. He was the only one that stayed firmly and courageously together with me, His Celestial Mother, at the foot of the Cross of my Son Jesus. Of all the apostles he was the strongest, despite his young age, because of his great love for God. And, Jesus put in him much of his trust, so much as to entrust me, the one whom He loved most in this world, to this young and small child's care. And your Celestial Mother has also showed how much She loves these little beloved children who so intensely need Her Maternal help: and chose them to manifest herself to men in her apparitions. I appeared and continue to appear many times to the children and to the youths, to show them that as Mother I always accompany all of my children, since their earliest childhood, teaching them the faith and the love of my Divine Son Jesus. I love all of them: children, youth and adults. They are all to me like fragile little children, and I receive and carry them in my maternal arms. I put all of them inside my Immaculate Heart to enrich them with uncountable graces, clothing them with my Immaculate light and preserving them from all stain that could harm the purity and light of their souls.

April 12, 1996

Everyone May Obtain What They Ask For…

Everyone may obtain what they ask for, through love and faith. Ask with faith and love in your hearts and you shall receive whatever you have requested… Whoever asks, whoever hopes in Jesus with his heart, shall receive everything.

April 19, 1996

This Terrible Sin Claims My Divine Justice

Many reject me in their hearts and in their life, committing the most abominable sins, for instance, the sins of impurity and the sins against nature. The number of abortions is excessively high here in Amazonas and in Brazil. This terrible sin claims my Divine Justice. Seek reparation for those terrible crimes, my children. Pray, fast and offer sacrifices and penitence to fix this terrible sin. Every parent should know how much this horrible sin hurts my Heart. My justice rests over murderous fathers and mothers, and not only over them, but also over all of those who promote these sins. No one escapes my justice. My justice sees everything and nothing goes unseen by my Holy eyes.

Dear souls, be modest and chaste in your outfits. Dress yourselves with decency, my daughters: without luxury but properly. My children, I don't want you attending my Church with exposed legs, as you have already be doing. Do not attend holy Mass while wearing shorts – wear pants that cover your legs. Many have adopted this habit of coming to my Church while wearing shorts. I do not want it to be this way: men have to wear trousers and women have to wear dresses. That is how it shall be.

April 27, 1996

What God Has Joined Together, Let No One Separate

On that day, early in the morning, my mother received a message from the Virgin, directed to the couples and to the families.

What God has united, let no one separate. Every religious marriage is blessed by God. Every man and woman makes a vow to God when they marry. Through this vow they will only separate them when one of them passes away. Every man and every woman has his/her freedom, but they must know how to live it.

Everyone is responsible for his or her freedom. Everyone will have to give an account to God one day. This message is directed to all the couples. For that reason I tell you now: every family belongs to My Family, and My Family belongs to all the families. Be aware: one day everyone is going to give an account to the Eternal Father.

I tell you: be a good tree to bear good fruits. As I also tell you: each person is responsible for his or her soul. That is all for today. I bless you: in the name of the Father, the Son, and the Holy Spirit. Amen. Amen!

June 2, 1996

Edson: This is one of the rare messages that the Eternal Father has deigned to transmit to my mother. When He talks to us, we feel so small, as a nothing in face of His Divine Majesty and Greatness. Who shall truly comprehend the great love that God has for His children? Only those, as Jesus tells us in the gospel, whom God wants to manifest and reveal it.

Eternal Father to Maria:

I am Your Beloved Father

Faith and confidence. Have much faith. Faith is a special gift that I have granted to each one of you. For that reason, pray to the Holy Spirit so that He may increase your faith. I come to bless you with all My Heart: in the name of the Father, the Son, and Holy Spirit. Amen.

Take my blessing to your families. I am the Lord, who loves you so much. I am your God and your Creator, who comes to pour His blessings upon all of you. Dear little children, have courage. Never be discouraged in your journey. I have you as my little children. I am your Beloved Father. Receive My merciful love, My eternal Love, which is so great. This sacred love is to all of you.

I am Peace, and I wish that my Peace be with you. Pray, pray and convert yourselves. I love you very much. Do not close your hearts, but open them up to my voice and listen to everything that I am telling you. I have many blessings for all of you. Pray, pray. I bless you: in the name of the Father, the Son, and the Holy Spirit. Amen. See you soon!

September 2, 1996

...You Easily Neglect Jesus in Your Hardships

Dear children, my message is a deep message of prayer and conversion. Be truthful in your acts and in your love for God, because He loves you unconditionally, and He is willing to help you in everything; but you easily neglect Jesus in your hardships and slip away from His hands, taking the path of sin.

September 29, 1996

My Children, Don't Reject These Holy Blessings

My beloved, my messages and secret revelations, yet to be unveiled are worth of respect. My messages are not for fun. What I tell you must be taken seriously. Men no longer care about God, and if they remain this way they will be lost in the way of darkness. My Immaculate Heart needs to be atoned. I seek for souls to console my Maternal Heart so offended and outraged.

My children, do not reject such holy blessings. Come to my Immaculate Heart and you shall find my Son Jesus Christ. I give you my blessing, a mother's blessing, my love to be taken to your brothers and sisters.

October 3, 1996

Be Unattached From Everything

Let go of everything. Pray, pray, pray. Jesus is the Peace. Try to enter into a deep silence within yourself. In the silence of your hearts you shall find God who conveys His grace, peace and love to you. I bless you with my maternal blessing, a blessing from a loving Mother.

October 12, 1996

Our Lady of the Sick

(In regard to a blessed fountain)

I want November 9th to be the day of Our Lady of the Sick in the State of Amazonas, here in the city of Itapiranga. And I also want that on each 9th day of every month the sick people be brought to bathe themselves and to drink water from the fountain of healing, whose name is: Fountain of Mercy and of Grace – or that their caregivers come to collect this water.

I also want that the priest of the city confess the sick, or that the ailing seek the priest to confess their sins. This recommendation is for the sick people of Itapiranga. The others who arrive here, are also to be prepared through confession.

The water from the fountain is for the people of the entire world. Any person may collect the water from the fountain, provided that he is not in state of mortal sin. Now, for those who are not prepared or are in the state of mortal sin, the water will not be effective.

October 26, 1996

Receive Me in Your Homes

Wherever my image goes, I shall pour abundant celestial blessings. Receive me in your homes my children, for I have received you in my Heart. Remain with my peace and my love. Remain with My Son Jesus.

October 27, 1996

Transmit My Immaculate Love to All My Children Around the World

My Divine Son has given me to you as your true Mother, and has given me all of you as my beloved children during His Holy Passion, when He was about to give His spirit to the Eternal Father, in His painful Crucifixion at Calvary.

Dear children, I desire to have you inside my Immaculate Heart. Transmit my immaculate love to all my children of the whole world. I wish to invite you to live a holy life, a life of love and peace amongst your brothers and sisters.

I am the Mother of Jesus, redeemer of the whole world, I wish to grant you my blessings. Receive them and distribute them among all my children. Always come to the arms of your Immaculate Mother. I love you. Pray, pray, pray. Pray the holy Rosary every day.

October 30, 1996

May the Rosary be Always in Your Hands as a Sign of Total Dedication to Me

My Son Jesus loves you very much. And you, my beloved, do you love Jesus with all your hearts? I invite you to live my holy messages. Whoever lives my celestial messages, makes my heart very happy. Pray the Rosary. May the Rosary be always in your hands as a sign of total surrender to me, your Celestial Mother. I bless you and I offer you my maternal love.

November 1, 1996

Live and Love the Holy Mass

The most important thing is that all of you have a deep experience of the Holy Mass with an open heart. Live and love the Holy Mass, for whoever loves and lives it, has God's blessing and disgrace shall never enter his dwelling place.

Our Lady made me understand that if we truly experience the Holy Mass, we shall be protected against all evil and perils. The Holy Mass is the sacrifice of Jesus on the Cross. It is the power of Love destroying the power of hatred and hell. There is nothing more powerful on earth than the Holy Mass and there will never be, because in the Mass Jesus is present, and Jesus is God, and while the Holy and Powerful name of Jesus is heard, every knee in Heaven, on earth and in hell shall bow down.

November 4, 1996

I Am Your Salvation

I love all of you. I have created and blessed all the creatures of the world. I am Jesus, your Savior. Remember, my beloved children, that I Am at your side in any need. I love you and I do not want your condemnation. I have not come to condemn you, to reprehend you, but to grant you my Love and forgiveness. Come to me. Come to my arms and I will conduct you through pastures, pure and green fields, and through rivers of crystal clear waters.

I am your Salvation. If you want peace, come to me and I will grant it to you. if you want love, come to me , for I am the living Love. If you want light, come to me, for I am the Light of the world. I give you my blessing, a blessing of peace and love, and in this place, I leave all of My love, merciful love to all of you and to my children of the whole world. Pray, pray, now, because I will mark you with My sign, the holy sign of the Cross. Those who carry this sign on their foreheads and keep it deep inside their souls with a profound and sincere repentance shall not see the eternal damnation, but the glory of Paradise.

Jesus marked us with a luminous cross on our foreheads. This does not mean that we can now possess Heaven forever, and do whatever we wish here on earth. It does not mean that. What Jesus did was to grant us a mammoth grace in order for us to live a holy and loving life and a life of conversion amid our brothers and sisters, observing the commandments and listening to the teachings of the Church, through the pope. If we put into practice all of this then the sign of the Cross marked on us by Jesus will have an immense and powerful value, because every time we do His will, we will have more strength and grace to be sanctified, to grow in faith, and to separate us definitively from a life of damnation and sin.

November 9, 1996

You are More Beautiful Than the Stars in the Sky

My children, do you think that the stars in the sky are beautiful?

They all responded: "yes!"

And she added:

But you are more beautiful than the stars in the sky, because the Holy Spirit lives in each one of you, for you were created in the image and likeness of God. For this reason, thank the Lord for having created you in such a beautiful manner. You are so beautiful, my children, and I love you very much.

December 8, 1996
Itapiranga is United to My Immaculate Heart

Families are being destroyed by the lack of communal prayer, and union of parents and children. I wish to advise you to seek refuge in my Immaculate Heart, thus being protected from all dangers and evil that the Enemy throws upon you at every moment. Itapiranga is united to My Immaculate Heart as it is united to all the other places where I have appeared and continue to appear nowadays. Itapiranga is another source of grace that I grant to the entire world.

December 10, 1996
Leave Your Sinful and Adulterous
Life Behind and Marry

This message is for all the people who live together as couple but are not married. I want them to get married as soon as possible, because they are on the way to hell, for they live in impurity and whoever lives in impurity lives in mortal sin. May all those who are not married, leave his/her sinful and adulterous life behind and marry, for I wish to see all of you on the path of sanctity.

December 11, 1996
Jesus to Maria do Carmo:

Whoever Loves Me, Loves My Mother!

Daughter, do you know why the people do not love Me? Because they live in mortal sin. Whoever loves me, loves My Mother!

December 12, 1996

Jesus to Maria do Carmo:

Fire That Shall Come Down From Heaven

Do not worry about the rain that is now pouring over you, be aware however of the fire that shall come down from Heaven, if mankind does not heed my appeals and convert.

December 15, 1996

Do Not Be Away From Me and From My Son

Dear children, my maternal love is for all of you. Do not depart from Me and from My Son Jesus. Come closer to us, so that our love, this pure, holy and eternal love, may protect you from all evil launched by the Enemy.

December 17, 1996

Jesus to Maria do Carmo:

Whoever Offends His Brother or Sister, Is Offending Me and My Mother

Daughter, do not be sad when people hurt you, slander you, insult you. Ultimately, my daughter, whoever offends his brother/ sister, offends Me and My Mother. Thanks for listening to me. I bless you: in the name of the Father, the Son and the Holy Spirit. Amen. Amen. Amen.

The Father, the Son, and the Holy Spirit are much offended, Maria do Carmo.

Jesus gave this message to my mother because we were receiving many reproaches, humiliations, and insults from the people of Itapiranga, specially from the priest… and from the people from within the Church. They criticized the apparitions and said absurd and distorted things, laughing and ridiculing the apparitions of Our Lady. People called us liars and crazy, they mocked us, among other things. It was not easy, but we bore everything with love and patience, for Jesus and for the Virgin´s sake. Whenever they said absurd things, I thought about the beautiful smile of the Virgin and about Her maternal words full of love – and everything was at ease within me, giving great peace to my heart. One day they will know the truth and will see that we are not lying. Our Lady really appears and talks to us. This has been and continues to be a great grace for me and for my mother, for my family, but I can also say it is a great grace for all the people of Amazonas.

December 17, 1996
Jesus to Maria do Carmo:

Do Not Speak Badly

When you cannot praise a person, do not speak ill of her either. Praising, yes, speaking ill, never! Unity yes, disunity, never.

December 24, 1996
Jesus and Our Lady to Maria do Carmo, in Manaus:

We Want All of You in Heaven With Us

My beloved children, you are highly loved by Me and my Son Jesus, we desire much peace in your hearts, and much joy in your lives and in the lives of your family members. I also ask that you pray more to drive the Enemy away from you and from the people of the whole world.

Our enemy is shrewd and has the power to do iniquities to the people, trying to steal the souls from My Son Jesus and lead them to hell. And this we do not desire, my children!

We want indeed all of you in Heaven with us. Therefore, pray with faith, every day, asking for your salvation. With faith ask for the light of the Holy Spirit, because those who have the Holy Spirit in their lives have everything in a special way.

Do not forget that today is Christmas Eve, the day before the Birthday of My Son Jesus Christ. On His birthday, He cries much with joy and also with sadness, because there are many people still suffering from hunger and other necessities. That is why you must also pray to end people´s sufferings. Do acts of charity, charity, as much as you can, for I promise a place in heaven for those who perform acts of charity. Thanks for hearing me. I bless you: in the name of the Father, the Son and the Holy Spirit. Amen. Amen.

December 25, 1996

Peace is the Main Theme of My Holy Messages

Priests, my favorite sons, pray, pray much. You must be an example to all the faithful. You must love your Church with a loving spirit, with a spirit of devotion, with a filial spirit. Carry a more pious life. Never allow your hearts to get closer to the ideas and things of the world. Your hearts should only long for the love of My Son Jesus. Only Jesus should be the goal of your life. Try to live a holy life in everything. You are the light that God grants to this sinful world. Mankind needs to see the Face of My Son Jesus reflected on yours. My sinful children are in great need of the Divine Mercy. For that reason you need to teach all of them to approach My Son Jesus, so that He can grant them His love and forgiveness.

Pray for peace, my children. Peace is the main theme of My holy messages. I am the Queen of Peace. I have come to the earth to call you to return to the Lord, through the path of conversion. Peace, peace, peace!

December 25, 1996

Apparition of the Three United
Hearts in One Love

It was Christmas day, a Wednesday, at 9:00 PM, and I was praying the Rosary. As I finished it, I had a very beautiful vision of Our Lady and St. Joseph with the Child Jesus. The three were dressed with the most pure golden garments, which tended to assume a clear tone.

Jesus and Our Lady showed their Holy Hearts and pointed with their hands to St. Joseph's Heart, who appeared surrounded by twelve white lilies, and inside of it, the cross of Christ and the "M" for Mary engraved in the form of a wound.

The twelve white lilies represented the purity and sacredness of St. Joseph's Heart, who has always been pure, chaste and who lived holiness at the highest level. It also represents the twelve tribes of Israel, of which St. Joseph reigns as the patriarch. The cross and the letter "M" for Mary engraved in the Heart of St. Joseph meant that St. Joseph loved and deeply imitated Jesus and Mary with His entire heart. They assumed an appearance of a wound because St. Joseph shared the sorrows of Jesus and Mary, with his pain, also participating in the ministry of redemption.

From the Hearts of the Child Jesus and the Virgin Mary came forth rays of light that went towards the Heart of St. Joseph. Those rays represented the one and triune love of the hearts of Jesus, Mary, and Joseph, as the Holy Trinity is one and triune in love.

The rays that are also departing from the hearts of Jesus and Mary and reflect in the heart of St. Joseph are to show us that St. Joseph imitated Jesus and Mary in everything and received all the blessings and virtues from their Most Holy Hearts. For Jesus and Mary shared everything with him and refused him nothing, in appreciation for the favors and services dedicated to both of them. Now, in retribution to so many aids, Jesus and Mary, in an extraordinary manner, ask that along with the devotion to their two Hearts, glorification and devotion be granted also to the heart of the one they have loved so much in this earth and now love eternally in heaven: St. Joseph.

The rays that depart from the heart of St. Joseph are all the graces and virtues, as well as all the pure and sacred love that he has received from the hearts of Jesus and Mary, and now he pours over all those who request his help and the grace from his Most Chaste Heart.

This triune devotion for the Hearts of Jesus, Mary and Joseph, united in one single love, glorifies the Holy Trinity, One and Triune, that has deeply poured His graces, blessings and virtues upon the Sacred Family of Nazareth.

Jesus Christ, Our Lord, and the Most Holy Virgin ask us that this devotion be put into practice, so that the Holy Spirit may effect, as soon as possible, the second Pentecost, pouring out His grace, His most pure light and the fire of His love upon the whole sinful humanity, already discouraged because of sin, and so granting her new life: sanctifying her totally as the Holy Family of Nazareth.

The Most Chaste Heart of St. Joseph comes to defend and protect with its help the devotion to the united Hearts of Jesus and Mary, as he has defended them from the persecution of their enemies while on earth.

Now, with the devotion to this Pure and Chaste Heart, the Lord asks the collaboration of St. Joseph, so that He will save the devotion to the Hearts of Jesus and Mary, destroying all the traps, persecutions, and attacks of Satan and his angels against her, protecting and defending her, as well as the Holy Church, with the blessings and grace that comes out of His Heart, during these last times of great fighting between good and evil.

> *My Glorious St. Joseph: take care of my family today, tomorrow and forever. Amen!*

December 27, 1996
Jesus to Maria do Carmo:

Every Person That Lives in
Adultery, Lives in Grave Sin

My daughter, Maria do Carmo, my peace be with all of you!

I tell you again: every person that lives in adultery lives in grave sin. Every man that lives with more than one woman, lives in a very grave sin, and the ones who live with more than two women or two men live in a graver state of sin. This means that such men and women are going straight to the path of hell and are against Me.

Sex is to be performed between two people that genuinely love each other, and should only happen after the religious wedding, in the Catholic Church, which is held in front of a priest, who represents Me. The civil union is to follow them in their conjugal lives, and warrants the right to material goods. The religious, or Catholic wedding, is to secure the right to heavenly goods. Sexual intercourse cannot happen: between a man and another man, a woman and another woman, or when there is consanguinity.[1] If one dies in the state of mortal sin, he/she will not escape hell, so flee from sin. Throw away all the dirt and return to me through confession and repentance, because without confession and repentance there is no forgiveness and without forgiveness there is no salvation. Thanks for heeding Me. I bless you: in the name of the Father, the Son and the Holy Spirit. Amen!

---

[1] When Jesus talked about consanguinity, He meant relationships between parents and children, uncles, aunts and nephews and nieces, brothers and sisters in law, mothers in law, and between cousins.

December 29, 1996

Jesus to Maria do Carmo:

My daughter, beloved by My Mother and Me, my peace be with all of you!

Every man, namely, every father, all mothers, every son and daughter that spend hours out of their homes, not working, or not doing something for the wellbeing of their families, or visiting someone who is in need, who are wasting money unnecessarily, while there are so many people hungry and in need in this world, I tell you: they are not worth of My Family. Thanks for listening to Me. I bless you: in the name of the Father, the Son, and the Holy Spirit. Amen!

MESSAGES OF 1997

January 1, 1997

I Have a Very Special Plan for the Families

Dear children,

I have a very special plan for the families. If all families live deeply my holy messages, soon many will be sanctified by Divine Grace. All families belong to the Heavenly Family, but will only remain faithful to it if they live in permanent union with God. God cherishes families and He blesses them through the heart of His Son Jesus, and the Immaculate Heart of His Heavenly Mother.

My daughters, mothers and wives, pray that Satan may not take possession of your homes, your husbands and children. You are responsible for them. Mothers and wives, God has a very special affection for you. Women's dignity is in being mothers. If mothers knew how precious the gift of motherhood is, they would never abort their children. Penance, penance, penance. Renounce sin with all your heart. Pray and you will be freed from sin.

January 2, 1997

You Still Don't Understand the Importance of Praying the Rosary

You still don't understand the importance of praying the Rosary. If you knew the value of praying the Rosary, you would pray it on a daily basis without ever failing. Many of my children are lazy to pray. Bear in mind, children, that laziness does not come from God. If you have not been able to renounce laziness, you should start now, so that God does not renounce you on the final days of your life, because laziness is a sin and sin drives you away from my Son Jesus Christ. Do not be lazy to pray, because if you keep praying, you will be leading the way toward salvation. Salvation is achieved only through prayer, man's effort and good will to do all that God asks for, through his holy Word and holy Church which, once again I tell you, is the Catholic Church.

Do Not Ever Permit My Tabernacles to be Profaned and Ravaged

Oh beloved children, do not ever allow my tabernacles to be ever profaned and ravaged, because of the great violations against my Church perpetrated by many of my children, who don't know how to value and respect my holy temple. It is the immodesty of many of my daughters, by wearing the most immoderate outfits when coming to my sanctuary, and thus hurting my Sacred Heart and tormenting me even more, increasing the pain of my Holy

Wounds. Oh my beloved children, care for the honor and glory of your God. Do not remain silent before such great desecration inside my Sanctuary. Warn my daughters about this great dishonor to their God. I Am the thrice Holy and I abhor any stain of sin. I desire to see all of you shining in sanctity. I desire to enrich you with my Divine Grace, beloved children. You are my worthy representatives. You are my anointed ones. You are loved by Me and my heavenly Mother in a special way. Blessed is the priest who has my Mother as his intercessor, and foremost, as his mother. I will not leave him unattended in his prayers, and in his most difficult times.

January 6, 1997

You Must First be Filial Souls of My Holy Mother

Now I tell you: before being charismatic souls, you must first of all be filial souls of my Holy Mother. Be united to Her so that, together with Her, you may receive through Her intercession, all graces that I wish to grant you for your spiritual growth and your own sanctification. Do not ever depart from Most Holy Mother so that you may always be led through My holy paths.

January 15, 1997

I Give You My Immaculate Heart…

Dear children, if you say that you love one another: do love one another, love one another. Dear children, you say that you love me, but you don't love your brethren yet. Live love, live peace, live in harmony among you. I am your Mother. I give you my Immaculate Heart…

Our Lady showed her Immaculate Heart.

January 25, 1997

Do Not Worry About the Persecutions

My son, do not worry about persecutions. They are necessary because it is through them that God renews and fortifies your faith. See how my Son Jesus suffered. He suffered greatly and was persecuted, until He died in a terrible way, even death on a cross. Accept your crosses, with patience and love.

Only a Priest has the Right and Grace
Given by God to Forgive Sins

Son, only a priest has the right and the grace given by God to forgive sins. Without confession there is no salvation. Children, know how to long for each creature God has created. Animals are to be treated with love and affection, because they are God´s creatures. But they should not be treated as if they were humans.

February 3, 1997

Faithfulness: the one who is faithful to my words I will never forget him on his trials nor on the last moment of his life.

I am the true Life. Give your lives to me so that you may be living people, not dead ones. Do you know what was my biggest proof of love?

At this point, I saw Jesus on the cross, on the moment of His crucifixion, on Mount Calvary, surrounded by a multitude of people mocking Him. Jesus prayed saying:

Father, forgive them because they don't know what they are doing. I love them, but they hate me. I forgive them, but they condemn me. I am here with opened arms to

receive them all, but they refuse to come to me. I want all
of you with me, by my side. I love you so!

During the prayer, I saw a hand with a ring on one of the
fingers. After a few moments this ring broke up, becoming
unusable. I asked Our Lady the meaning of this vision, to
what She answered:

These are marriages destroyed by man and woman's
unfaithfulness, who do not fulfill the vows done before
God's Altar, before my Son Jesus, when they got married.
Warn all couples about this serious fault: of not being
faithful to this vow that they have made before my Son
Jesus, at the time of their wedding.

February 11, 1997

Dear children, I come to tell you that the times of great
darkness for the Church are approaching. How painful,
dear children, it is to tell you this: evil men will persecute
my poor and dear favorite children until they bleed. Many
will be martyred for their love of God and of the Holy
Church. I wish to tell all my sons who are priests that I
am with them, at their side, to receive their sacrifice and
immolation. I present all of them before God every day so
that my Lord will strengthen them in faith and love.

February 15, 1997

My children: whoever loves me, loves his neighbor. Never
hold grudges in your hearts. He who loves me, keeps my
commandments. Children, he who truly loves Me and my
Most Blessed Mother does not love the world any longer,
because the world for these persons is no longer of major
importance. Whoever loves my Word is the one who shines
in my presence, for he is a strong light illuminating all the
other little ones of mine who are in darkness. Satan tries

*at any cost to destroy this holy work that I and my Most
Holy Mother have started in Amazonas. Be careful. Keep
watching. Be on the alert for those messages that do not
teach the truth proclaimed by the authority of My Holy
Church, which is the Catholic Church. The messages of
Satan are bitter, sour and do not bear fruits. Fruits may
only arise and increase abundantly when the messages
come only from Me and from my Holy Mother. Pray,
pray, pray that Satan departs from all of you. I wish only
peace and union. Pray, pray much.*

February 17, 1997

*Seek me not only in those persons whom you love, but
also in those persons that mistreat and persecute you. My
apostles ought to live out of love, because I love everyone
without distinction.*

The reading of the Scripture that Jesus gave to the group that
afternoon was the following: Hebrews 13:1-3:

"Keep yourself in fraternal charity. Do not forget hospitality,
by which some have sheltered angels without knowing it.
Remember those in prison as if you yourselves were with
them in prison. And of those mistreated, as if you dwelt in
the same body."

February 19, 1997

*My dear children, I am here sent by my Divine Son to free
you from all anguishes and evils. Come to my Motherly
arms so that I can grant you the peace that my Divine Son
Jesus offers through my Immaculate Heart. Pray, pray,
pray and keep the recitation of the Rosary, daily, so that
peace may come to the whole world.*

February 24, 1997

Dear children, pray much for all families. Many families are being destroyed because my Enemy has sown division, loneliness, intrigue and many sad things in many homes. You are responsible for praying for them. I bless you all and tell you this: ask for peace for the families and for the intercession of my Most Holy Mother, because I have designated Her Queen of all families. I invite you to return to Me with all your hearts.

Ask always for the gift of fortitude, so that you may be able to proclaim my Word with a firm and strong voice, and that you be steadfast in the fulfillment of my Word and my Will. Many are called, but few are chosen: many are called to live my Word, but few remain faithful to It. Pray for one another. Cheer up. Help those who are falling to rise up!

February 26, 1997

My dear daughters, mothers and wives, take care of your children with a loving heart. Your children are the most precious jewels that God has granted you. Bless them always, and never let the wickedness of this world approach them. How can this take place? By allowing your children to learn the worst things that are broadcast today on TV. The television is an evil idol that man have created to serve the Enemy, instead of God. If they knew how to use the means of communication to build the kingdom of God, that would be great. But today, men just use it for the progress of the evil in the world. Pray for all those that teach horrible and wrong things to all children, for they will not escape the Divine Justice, because they are destroying my Son Jesus' little angels in this world.

March 1, 1997

Dear children, I beg you: flee from sin. Do not search for God in places where His word is not correctly lived. Truth is only found in the Catholic Church. Many errors are spread throughout the world because people no longer pray to Holy Spirit asking for enlightenment. Pray to the Holy Spirit and He will show you the Truth. Do not ask me so many questions, but rather listen to Me. The current times are not very good. Urgent conversion of all peoples is necessary. I invite all of you: come back to God, truly.

March 3, 1997

Families whose foundation is upon the world will never remain standing. Families whose foundation is based on God and His love will remain standing and intact, and my Enemy will not approach them. Pray, always my children:

Oh Holy Family of Nazareth, Jesus, Mary, and Joseph, on this moment we truly consecrate ourselves to You, with all our hearts. Protect and defend us against the evils of this world so that our homes may always be steady on God´s infinite love. Jesus, Mary and Joseph, we love you with all our hearts. We want to be all yours. Help us to do the will of the Lord, truly. Guide us always to heavenly Glory, now and forever more. Amen!

March 4, 1997

Modesty and Chastity

My peace I give to all of you!

I say it again: I want you to be respectful when you pray in this place, or when you gather together with the people to pray. Be well-dressed, also receive those who are well-

dressed, that is, men are to wear long pants and sleeve
shirts; women shall be wearing a dress or a skirt. Dresses
and blouses are to be with sleeves. The longer the better.
Women's garments should be loose to the body. When they
wear clothes tight to the body, they look like a snake, of a
poisonous kind.

Women are not advised to use pants and shorts, but when
they do use them, they should be loose to the body and, the
shorts are to be below the knees; and men's are to be to the
knees. These kinds of clothes are fitting when you are at ease
at home, or traveling, or at the beach, whereas when at
Church in prayer or in prayer groups, you should all dress
modestly and with no ostentation: as simple as possible.
Thank you for answering us. We bless you: in the name of
the Father, the Son, and of the Holy Spirit. Amen!

March 8, 1997

Dear children, the knowledge of a person's future belongs
to God alone. Watch out for those who claim to predict
somebody's future because they do not act in the name of
God, but of Satan. Only God can know, should know and
does know one's destiny, and no one else. Pray, pray, pray
that God may deliver all of you from evil and the terrible
errors that have spread to the whole world today.

March 15, 1997

Dear children, I invite you to do penance. Do more
penance and dedicate part of your day to prayer. Jesus still
waits for you, and so do I. Dear children, do not depart
from Me. Leave pride behind and live my Holy messages.
Only those who are humble are able to know how and
listen to My voice. Ask God to teach you His Most Holy
Will, and not yours own. You do not yet fulfill God's will

because you haven't truly given yourselves to Me. Do not hurt my Motherly Heart. Do not let me shed tears because of your obstinacy. Obey me. I ask nothing for myself, but it is for your own good that I ask you to come back, do come back, come back, because the time for conversion is running out.

March 16, 1997

Our Lady to Maria do Carmo:

May my peace be with all of you! My daughter Maria do Carmo, propagate, propagate, propagate this message to the whole world: whoever offends and humiliates someone here on earth, it is Me and My Son Jesus Christ that he offends and humiliates. Thank you for answering Me. I bless you in the name of the Father, of the Son, and of the Holy Spirit. Amen! Amen!

March 25, 1997

Our Lady to Maria do Carmo:

May my peace be with all of you! Tell all sinners: come back, come back, come back as soon as possible. I tell you over and over again: convert, flee from vices, despise sin. Sin, my little children, is the enemy of my Son Jesus. That is why My Son and I cry so much, tears of blood. Don't be afraid to come back to Jesus, who alone is your Savior and the Savior of the whole world.

Humanity has not yet entrusted itself to God. So many years have gone by and many people still do not mind about the Father, the Son and the Holy Spirit. Why so much disobedience, little children of mine?

I am the Queen of Peace and your heavenly mother. I am very much concerned about all those who don't care about my presence here on the Earth. I come to you for a special reason: to warn you, for your salvation.

I tell you again, come back to my Son Jesus because He is everything in your life. Thank you for answering Me. I bless you in the name of the Father, of the Son, and of the Holy Spirit. Amen. Amen.

April 3, 1997

Our Lady to Maria do Carmo:

My peace to all of you, children of mine! Ask for daily forgiveness for the faults you have committed, especially this year. This is not only the year of the family, but it is also the year to forgive and to ask for forgiveness.

Father and mother, ask your children's forgiveness for the faults you have committed. Children ask your parent's forgiveness for the faults you have committed.

Each person must ask his brethren for forgiveness of the wrongs committed. You must ask for forgiveness and always forgive when they commit transgressions.

Thank you for answering me. I bless you in the name of the Father, of the Son, and of the Holy Spirit. Amen. Amen, Jesus!

Jesus to Maria do Carmo:

I also bless you in the name of the Father, of the Son, and of the Holy Spirit. Amen. Amen!

Jesus told my mother, sorrowful and sadly:

Daughter, when I see so many perversities in the world, My Heart breaks in many pieces and it hurts very much.

Cherish me before the Most Blessed Sacrament of the altar. Say this:

Heavenly Father, I love You. Lay here on my shoulder. I want to cherish you and to ask for forgiveness for all those who do not know how to cherish you and make an apology to You. Forgive me, Lord. Amen.

April 14, 1997
St. Michael the Archangel to Edson:

Peace from the Lord and Our Most Holy Virgin to all of you!

I am St. Michael the Archangel and I come to you, at the request of Jesus and the Most Holy Mary. Jesus wishes that all of you receive His Most Holy Mother with much love and affection, and that you recite the prayer I am going to teach you now:

"Oh Mary, Virgin Most Holy and Immaculate, bless us and protect us against all evil. Right now we truly entrust ourselves to You, heart, soul and body. Oh Mother of God, be our salvation now and on the last moment of our life. Lead us to Jesus and pray for us to Our Lord that He may give us His Peace and Love. Amen!"

Pray, pray, pray. This is a request from the Virgin Mother. I bless you all on behalf of the Lord and of the Virgin Mary, in the name of the Father, of the Son, and of the Holy Spirit. Amen. Amen! See you soon!

June 6, 1997

Children of mine, I love you so. Men have not yet understood the infinite value of My love for them. If you knew how much love I have for you, you would cry for joy. I am your Eternal Salvation, the Source of Mercy and Grace.

My children, always try to feel Me close to you through prayer, prayed from the heart. I seek in the whole world for a soul that wishes to faithfully serve Me, but I find only a few. My children, do not waste so many graces. I come from heaven to place you all into My Sacred Heart. If you want to receive graces, you must have unlimited trust in My Sacred Heart. Ask anything with faith, you will receive it. Love, love, love. The more you love, the more you will receive from Me, whatever you ask for.

I desire that the first Wednesday, after the Feast of my Sacred Heart and the Immaculate Heart of Mary, be dedicated to the Feast of the Most Chaste Heart of St. Joseph.

I understood that it was the Wednesday following these two Feasts of the Sacred of Heart of Jesus and the Immaculate Heart of Mary. On that year, the feast of the Sacred Heart of Jesus was on June 6th; the feast of the Immaculate Heart on June 7th; and the feast of the Most Chaste Heart of St. Joseph was on Wednesday, June 11th. It was the first time Jesus revealed to me the day of the feast of the Most Chaste Heart of St. Joseph. We celebrated this feast at the Church of the Sacred Family in Ghiaie di Bonate, as I was in Italy with Father Vincenzo Savoldi.

June 8, 1997

My Immaculate Heart Is Your Refuge for Protection

My little ones, you are to be a living light shining God's Love in this world. Your lives are to be holy and pure. God has plans of mercy for all of you.

Dear youth, my Immaculate Heart is your refuge for protection. Consecrate everyday your thoughts, your bodies, and your souls to God, so that He may protect you against all evil. Live a life of faith. Always have confidence in God and also in My Immaculate Heart. Dear youth, open your hearts to Jesus. May your hearts burn with love for Jesus, so that He may mold your hearts transforming them totally.

June 11, 1997

The Whole World Should Have a Great Love for the Most Chaste Heart of St. Joseph

Dear children, when I appeared in Ghiaie di Bonate with Jesus and St. Joseph I wanted to show you that later on the whole world should have a great love to the Most Chaste Heart of St. Joseph and to the Holy Family, because Satan would attack the families very profoundly in this end of times, destroying them. But I come again, bringing the graces of God Our Lord, to grant them to all the families most in need of Divine protection.

Jesus conveyed the following message:

Love, love, love the Most Chaste Heart of My Virginal Father Joseph. Give yourself totally to this Pure, Most Chaste and Virginal Heart, because My Sacred Heart has shaped it to be My vessel of graces to sinful humanity, as the Immaculate Heart of My Mother, the Most Holy Mary.

He who has a deep devotion to the Most Chaste Heart of St. Joseph will not be eternally lost. This is the great promise, which I do here in this Holy place.

On this day, St. Joseph sent me his message:

The Divine Savior and My Spouse the Most Blessed Mary allow me to grant you all graces. I will pray intensely to Jesus and Mary for you.

Then, the three said together:

We, the Holy Family, bless you: in the name of the Father, of the Son, and of the Holy Spirit. Amen. Farewell!

June 12, 1997
Our Lady to Maria do Carmo:
Come Back While There Is Still Time

My peace to all of you!

I am sad and ashamed of those who stifle my messages. My messages are divine things. They are things that come from heaven to be spread to all Christians all over the world.

That is where the blind, the deaf and the dumb are: Many people do not want to see, hear and speak about God´s things, but the things of the world, and of God's Enemy, everyone sees, hears, speaks and puts them into practice. That is why you should pray very intensely and faithfully. Flee from worldly things and return to My Son Jesus Christ. I beg you: come back while there is still time, for time passes and never comes back. Thank you. Thank you for answering me. I bless you: in the name of the Father, the Son and of the Holy Spirit. Amen. Amen!

June 12, 1997

Do Not Fear Daily Difficulties, But Know How to Overcome Them

The path that leads to Jesus is narrow, but you all can follow it with confidence because I am with you to help and guide you through it.

Children, do not fear daily difficulties, but know how to overcome them with confidence and joy. Pray, pray, pray.

June 13, 1997

Do Penance

Dear children, do penance. Ask God to renew your hearts. Free yourselves, dear children, from all sin. Dear children, take away all sorrow and all hatred from your hearts. If you want to be of God, love, because God is love. You must live out of love. Love is something so wonderful, my children, because it is Jesus who pours His graces upon you and He is in you.

May the Priests be Pure and Holy

"What do You have to say to the priests?"

May the priests be pure and holy. The priests have received the divine mission to bring Jesus to all men through the Holy Sacraments. Jesus is vividly present in the Holy Sacraments, granting them His love and His graces in the Holy Eucharist, His forgiveness in the Holy Sacrament of Confession, because He earnestly desires your eternal salvation.

I invite you tonight to pray much for the neediest souls in purgatory. Pray, pray, pray.

Live the Word of God deeply. Spread the devotion to the Holy Hearts to your brothers and sisters.

Pray for those children who are in danger of being aborted from their mothers' womb. Fathers and mothers who abort their children are no longer human persons, but true images of Satan because abortion is a demonic work in the world.

May all the youths seek to live a life of intimate union with Jesus, so that Jesus may give them the strength and grace necessary to overcome the snares of Satan. Tonight your Heavenly Mother blesses you with the blessing of peace: in the name of the Father, the Son and of the Holy Spirit. Amen. See you then!

June 18, 1997

Always be Prepared

Dear children, I want the individual conversion of each one of you. Your conversion should be daily. You do not know the day or the hour when the Lord will call you to Him, so be prepared, with the soul clean from every stain of sin.

The love from My Immaculate Heart is for all of you. Ask the Lord to heal the wounds that sin has inflicted upon your souls. If you want to be the Lord's, live a life of prayer, sacrifice and penance. I pour upon you the flame of love from my Immaculate Heart, so that your hearts may be inflamed by the love of my Lord.

July 1, 1997

Come Even Closer to the Sacred Heart of Jesus

The most important thing, dear children, is that you all come closer to the Sacred Heart of Jesus. This is the goal of my many apparitions in the world. If you do not go to Mass, neither confess, and do not live the Gospel of Jesus, loving and helping your brethren, you will not be doing anything. Therefore I invite you to return to the path of conversion that I am preparing for you, and then you will be able to reach Jesus.

July 2, 1997

Pray for all Those People who Commit Adultery

You still are not able to be profoundly united with God because of your weakness of falling into various sins. Flee from all sin, so that the Grace of my Lord may be expanded in your lives.

Children, pray for all those who commit adultery. They do not know how dangerous this sin is. If people do not sincerely renounce this sin, asking the Lord for forgiveness, they will be in danger of being lost forever. Do not allow sin to destroy your souls. Tonight, meditate deeply on this message of mine: you still have many weaknesses that make it impossible for you to understand my Motherly love and God's love, because you are attached to worldly things. Pray, pray, pray and you will be free from all slavery of sin and, thus, God's love will transform you wholly.

July 3, 1997

Do not Let Sin Blind you

My children, do not let sin blind you. Many have eyes, but they do not see, ears, but do not hear, because they have abandoned God. If you knew the value of eternity, you would fight daily, without ever fainting, to achieve it. I am here among you, with all my Motherly presence to lead you to Jesus.

July 4, 1997

Be People of Prayer

Dear children, be people of prayer. Satan destroys many souls because they have abandoned prayer. If you want to be of God, you should strive to know Him more deeply through prayer, because it is through prayer that the Lord transforms your hearts. I invite you to renounce sin and to accept again the path of prayer, sacrifice and penance, because only thus you will be able to gain Paradise. May your lives be rays of light that illumine this world of darkness, and may your hearts be truly holy tabernacles, where God may pour out His love and His peace.

July 5, 1997

Do Not Lose Your Faith

My children, do not lose your faith. The Lord always grants it, all you have to do is ask with faith and He will grant it for you. It is necessary that you all pray to the Holy Spirit. Do not forget that you all need the divine light and the gift of fortitude, so that you may overcome all temptations with tranquility, without ever faltering. Tonight I pray for each one of you and ask the Lord to cover you with His Divine Love. God is Love, therefore, dear children, if you love your brethren and those who mistreat you, you will be truly the image of God, in this world that does not live love.

July 6, 1997

Dearest Daughters, Mothers, and Wives

Dear children, tonight I especially bless all mothers and My Son Jesus blesses in a special way all my other children.

Dearest daughters, mothers and wives, I turn once again to all of you: you must live a profound life of prayer and consecrate yourself every day to my Immaculate Heart, as well as your families, so that you may be protected by my Lord, Who has entrusted me to you to be your protector and the Queen of your families.

Daughters, fear nothing before me, even though your homes are being violently attacked by my Enemy. I tell you: I am here to protect you all. I ask you for an unlimited trust in my Motherly protection.

I love you, I love you, I love you, my dear children. If you want to know deeply my Motherly love and the love of My Son Jesus, you must surrender yourself to us without reservation, because we truly surrender ourselves to you with all our love. Pray, pray and you may understand the value of our presence among you. Be faithful to my Son Jesus. Do not let His Sacred Heart grieve seeing you falling into serious sin. This is my request and my message tonight.

July 8, 1997

Tell Everyone to Always Pray the Holy Rosary

Dear children, pray, pray, pray. Tell everyone to pray the Holy Rosary always, for it is with this prayer that we will change the most difficult situations that are affecting the whole world today. Know how to give to prayer a great value. It is the most effective weapon that God gives you in any difficult situation and obstacle that arises in your lives.

Dear children, if you live my messages, you will help me to accomplish the triumph of my Immaculate Heart in the world more and more, and especially in the hearts of your

*brethren, for all will know the love of my son Jesus, they
will feel His peace and then be converted.*

July 9, 1997

Seek the Forgiveness and Love of Your God

*Dear children, do not allow Satan to turn you away from
your resoluteness to converting. Do not be discouraged and
do not despair when, for some reason, you fall into any
error, but above all seek the forgiveness and love of your
God, for He is the Infinite Mercy, and always forgives you
when He sees in you the resolve of amending yourself, and
the desire of being better each day.*

July 10, 1997

All of You are Being Called by Me

*My little ones, I wish to give you all of my love. For those
who are here, I tell you that you are my special guests to
listen to this Holy Message of mine. Everyone is special to
me, but as I told you: many are called, but few are chosen.
All of you are being called to conversion by me, through my
Holy Mother. It is necessary that you do not harden your
hearts, so that I may always have you with me, united to
my Sacred Heart.*

Come to Me for the Time of
Mercy is Running Out

*Little children, wake up, wake up. As I have already
told you: woe to those who mocked and outraged my Holy
Mother, her apparitions and her holy messages. They will
have to settle an account with me one day. And I say to
you that, on that day when they will settle an account
with me, they shall not find me as a Merciful God, but*

a God of justice, for my justice is also great. If you want my mercy and my love, do not miss the opportunity, my little children. I easily forgive you if you sincerely ask for forgiveness and if you repent of your acts, but hurry up; come to me, for the time of Mercy is running out. I tell you that if it had not been for my Holy Mother and her apparitions in the world asking for My Mercy and Love, my Divine Justice would have already fallen upon you a long time ago. But for the prayers of my Mother, once again Mercy overcame justice.

July 11, 1997

Love Does Great Wonders

Children, it is only with Love that you may receive everything from my Son Jesus. That is why I ask you again: love, love, love. Love does great wonders. With love, dear children, you can receive even great miracles from my Son Jesus. The more you love, the more you will receive graces from My Son Jesus. Therefore, dear children, may your lives be lived in union with love and that your hearts become furnaces of burning love.

July 12, 1997

Be an Example to Your Brothers and Sisters

Dear children, here is My message tonight: be an example to your brothers and sisters, so that God, through each one of you, may pour out His Divine grace on all hearts that are still hardened, totally transforming them in true holy temples of peace and love where He may dwell. Do not give up, my little children, the resolve to follow the path of conversion, but confidently walk toward the Lord. I am here to help you.

July 13, 1997

I Shed From My Eyes Tears of Blood

Beloved children, do much penance and many sacrifices. It is necessary that all of you pray for all the Holy Church. I tell my sons priests that they should live a pure and holy life, because my Lord has a great love for each one of them.

Dear children, I beseech you: sin no more! Many times my eyes shed bloody tears because my children commit grave sins. Flee from sin, my children. I come to you for a very serious reason. If you do not convert, you must soon experience great trials.

August 2, 1997

The Most Beautiful Gift

If you want to give me a gift on August 5th, the most beautiful gift would be to see you united as true brothers and sisters, living peace and love among you. Love, love, love, otherwise you will only bring unhappiness to yourselves.

May you dedicate yourselves this week to help those who have been cause of disagreement and loneliness to others and to their families.

May you be united to the person who has difficulty to communicate and to love. To all a very affectionate Mother's blessing. I bless you and invite you to be a light in this world, and not an obstacle in the conversion of your brethren.

Pray for the End of Violence

Dear children, pray for the end of violence. My Immaculate Heart is sad because in men there is shortage of love and peace. Many destroy each other so brutally that they make me shed tears of blood. It is necessary that you love each other in union with Jesus. I desire love, love, love. Remain united to my Motherly Heart and Jesus will grant you all graces.

August 9, 1997

Adore and Love Jesus

If you want to be with me one day in paradise, so that together we may praise, adore and love Jesus, it is necessary that you listen to my maternal pleas. Trust God and also me, for we want to be with each one of you to help you in everything. Think that God created you for a world of peace and love, and not to live in hatred and loveliness. You are responsible for renewing this pagan world, transforming it into a new world full of God's love, because Jesus is with every person who wants to work to build a better world. Live the message of peace: peace, peace, peace!

August 23, 1997

All Young People Listen to My Appeals

Only those who truly love will live in the glory of Paradise, because in Heaven one only lives out of love. Therefore, dear children, during this week may you live the love with those in your homes and with all those you meet on a daily basis.

I want to gather all the young people in my love and in the love of my Son Jesus. I wish that all young people listen to my appeal, so that they will suffer less and achieve true happiness in this world, and then they will forever be in heaven next to Me and Jesus.

You will never find happiness in vices, in worldly pleasures, but only in my Son Jesus. Only in Him you will be truly holy and pure people.

Pray for all those who despise the truths taught by God, and never stop a single minute to meditate on the Passion of my Son Jesus and all that He had to endure to save you from eternal damnation. Pray, pray, pray and I will pray with all of you.

September 6, 1997
I Beg all Priests to Listen to My Call

May the priests be holy, truly holy, because God is thrice Holy, and He desires that His ministers live sanctity and spread it wherever they go. A priest who does not pray and live the daily prayer united to God does not fulfill His Will.

Priests ought to live the prayer intensely, because it is in prayer that Lord God grants them the graces and the light necessary to faithfully lead His flock.

I beg all priests to listen to my call. Only in this way they will be able to solve the most difficult problems and will have the necessary strength to carry out the mission that Jesus assigned to them. It is through prayer united to God that they may even be able to perform wonderful deeds and obtain great miracles from the Heart of Jesus.

September 14, 1997
Jesus to Maria do Carmo:
I am Patient, but do not Abuse

My peace to you all!

Whoever does not love me with sincerity, obedience, and respect will never possess happiness on earth or in Heaven. I am patient, but do not wear out my patience. I love all My children. Therefore, I ask: sincerity, obedience and mutual respect towards me. Thank you for paying heed to me. I bless you: in the name of the Father of the Son and of the Holy Spirit. Amen. Amen!

September 15, 1997

My children, once again I invite you to remain united: if you are not in harmony you will never be able to understand My love.

I ask you to never judge or criticize anyone, because when you do so, you are not pleasing My Immaculate Heart.

Never look at the faults of your brethren, but try to improve yours, because today, many are those who only take notice of other's faults.

September 16, 1997

I Invite You to the Union

My children, if you pray with a living faith, you will obtain from me and from My Lord special graces. Pray, pray, pray and pray, you will understand what you should do and how you should act in your daily life. I am united to you in prayer and I dedicate myself daily for your salvation. You are receiving so many graces and still do not know how to appraise them.

September 18, 1997

Little children, when you go to the place where the chapel is built, try to enter into a spirit of deep prayer and union with God, because in that place, the Lord pours out abundant graces, which your minds are not able to conceive. I Am in that place, along with my Son Jesus, with many graces to pour upon all those who faithfully ask with a firm purpose of conversion. Pray, pray, pray, because in prayer, God longs to lead you to the path of perfect love and full sanctity. With deep contemplation in your hearts spend these days as a true spiritual retreat for your souls, for I will be enlightening and helping you.

September 19, 1997

My children, know how to value everything that I, and My Holy Mother, have started here at Itapiranga. If all of you live our petitions, then multitudes of souls will find the road to salvation. Ponder on this message of Mine. It is to be known by all My children. I come to give you the grace of My love and mercy to all My sinful children.

October 5, 1997

May all Families be a True Example of God's Love

It is necessary to combat with God´s power the crimes committed against the dignity of the families. Never allow your families to be led by wrong values propagated by the media, but may all men know how to use these means to spread the Gospel of My Son Jesus in the hearts of those who do not yet know God´s love.

My little children, may all families be a true example of God's love and His Holy Image in the world. God sends me from Heaven to bestow upon all Brazilian families and those of the whole world His heavenly graces and blessings, and to tell them to listen to the voice of His representatives in the world. If they do so, families will be saved from destruction, but if they remain deaf, the consequences may be huge and worse.

October 6, 1997
Our Lady to Maria do Carmo:

Everything can be Changed by My Son, Jesus

The peace of My Son Jesus and My Peace to all of you!

I am your Heavenly Mother and I come to warn you once more. I am very worried about what is going to happen to the world if you do not pray with faith and love in your heart.

Everything can be changed by My Son Jesus, if you obey my appeals. Change is for the good of all people of the whole world. If they do not obey, humanity's suffering will be terrible. That is why I ask you to obey. Thank you for answering me!

I bless you all: in the name of the Father, the Son and the Holy Spirit. Amen. See you soon!

October 7, 1997
Our Lady to Edson:

I Beg You to Abandon the Path of Pride and Falsehood

Peace be with you!

Dear children, as your Mother, I come to you from Heaven to tell you to live the love and unity in your homes and with all those you encounter on a daily basis.

My children, I beg you to abandon the path of pride and falsehood. Do not be hypocrites, but true people with a pure and simple heart. Among my true apostles there is no self-interest, but the will to serve everybody with an open heart.

I pray to God for you, asking Him for the grace for you to understand my messages and my Motherly love. Listen to me, because God still allows me to speak to you. Live every Holy Mass immersed in the love of God and deeply adoring the Sacred Heart of My Son Jesus. I bless you all: in the name of the Father, the Son and the Holy Spirit. Amen. See you soon!

October 8, 1997

Jesus:

Do Not be Impatient with Trials

Dear children, do not be impatient in the face of trials. You must remain steadfast, for My true apostles should never grow weak. I am your Strength, so why do you fear?

Be pure and holy always. I still hope for your conversion and the sincere conversion of all humanity and I will never be tired of alerting you, because my Heart cares about you.

Come back to me, My children, for I am with open arms to welcome you. May this message remain in your hearts.

October 11, 1997

Live in Your Families with Peace and Unity

Tonight, I beg you to live in your families with peace and unity.

Dear children, you must be closely united, because when you are united, God is present. I pray to God that He may grant you the gift of love and peace.

Dear children, pray much for the conversion of sinners. Many are those who get lost in sin and cause my Heart to bleed.

Pray, pray, pray and cling to God's works. Jesus wants to save you from all evil. Listen to Me: He died to save you from eternal death. It was by His Holy Passion that you were redeemed, therefore, dear children, may the wounds of my Son Jesus become for each one of you the means to obtain eternal salvation. Honor them in your lives and you all will be God's.

October 12, 1997

The Importance of Confession

Dear children, today I wish to talk to you about the importance of confession. If you do not confess regularly you will be in danger of being lost eternally. Many do not approach the Sacrament of Confession to sincerely ask for forgiveness of their sins and this worries me, because these children of mine are far from the Heart of My Son Jesus and from My Immaculate Heart.

Dear children, many are those who confess only by habit, but remain the same afterwards. Convert deeply and repent from your sins.

I am united here, vividly present, and I look at each of you with Motherly tenderness. I am your Mother and I want to help you in your needs and afflictions.

October 13, 1997

I ask all my children priests to be, first of all, model and example, for all my other children in the faith.

Priests, listen to me: I am your Queen and the Mother of God and I come to help you to faithfully fulfill the mission that My Son Jesus entrusted to you.

My children, today you are celebrating My last apparition at Fatima, to My three little shepherds. So many years ago, I spoke at Fatima, giving My message, but men remain deaf. They do not want to obey what the Lord has recommended through Me. I tell you, that now as never before, listening to my Motherly appeals has become more imperative, because difficult moments are approaching you, my children. Punishments will come in greater proportions if you do not convert. Humanity is destroying itself more and more with the leprosy of sin.

Children, wake up. Live my messages. I want to save you from these tribulations. I come not to frighten you, but to warn them.

October 20, 1997
Jesus to Edson:

My Holy Message That is Destined for all the Priests

Tonight, Jesus directed me to a passage from the Holy Scriptures: Isaiah 56: 9-12; 57: 4.

Come, my dear son, write my holy message that is destined to all the priests. Do not waste time and pay attention to all that I will say about the reading that has been given to you. Today my priests are as asleep. A thick darkness surrounds many of my favorite children. Some of them have let themselves be involved in darkness, because they did not have a life of intimate union with Me, even though being priests of my Church. Look at my Church! From heaven I see My Church so desolate, living moments of great confusion and even of great rebellion. There are many who no longer have faith. They are with their hearts as cold as ice. There is no one who is willing to listen to me, through My Church and especially through the voice of My representative in the world, the pope ... Children priests, listen to the voice of your God. Remain faithful to the pope. You must be to the sheep entrusted to you a sign of holy example and obedience. Woe to the priests who did not know how to care for the flock entrusted to them. Woe to the bad priest, the one who cared more about his own interests and the things of the world than about My interests and the things of heaven. To these priests my Divine Justice is weighing heavily, if they do not sincerely repent of their faults.

"But Lord, if they repent, will they be forgiven?"

Yes, if they repent, they will receive My forgiveness. But it is necessary that all listen to this My appeal to them. Many have become deaf, they have closed their hearts because they no longer want to free themselves from worldly things and their wrong doings, and thus stifle My voice, which calls them to return and repent. They stifle My voice that speaks to them inside their hearts. Favorite children, have you not realized that you are united with Me through the priesthood? Then why do you make Me suffer so much with your betrayals, like Judas who betrayed Me, often committing terrible sins? To My consolation, I still have a number of priests who remain faithful to My precepts and teachings, and are obedient to My voice and to the voice of my beloved Pope. Through this message I call all priests to return to Me in faithfulness, renewing their promise to remain committed to their apostolic mission. To all my favorite children My Holy Blessing, that they may ask, through the intercession of the Immaculate Heart of my Holy Mother and of the Most Chaste Heart of my Virginal Father St. Joseph, the grace of being true examples of holiness for all the faithful.

I bless my children priests of the world over: in the name of the Father, the Son and the Holy Spirit. Amen!

Jesus taught two prayers for the priests:

Lord, sanctify all priests by the merits of Your Holy Passion, so that they may be your true image, pure and holy in the world. Amen!

Lord, by the bitterness you felt for Judas' treacherous kiss, bring back to the sanctifying grace all the priests who were unfaithful to their vocation and who remain obstinate in the sins of the world. This we ask through the intercession of the Immaculate Heart of Mary and of the Most Chaste Heart of St. Joseph. Amen!

Messages of 2001

January 1, 2001

The World Will be Renewed and a New Dawn of Peace Shall Take Place

Peace be with you!

Dear children, I am the Mother of God and I bless each one of you. O how I love you! Today I bless you with a blessing of peace. I am the Queen of Peace. God, Our Lord, has sent Me from Heaven to bestow upon you His holy blessings and His message of peace. I come down from Heaven because God loves you.

Little children, a new year begins. How joyful I am to see that you start this new year with God. Jesus is granting a special blessing for your families. Jesus can solve even the most difficult problems, if you trust Him.

My Immaculate Heart is overjoyed for seeing you here. Today I bless the whole world. It was here, dear children, at this place, that your Celestial Mother appeared for the first time. And it is right here, that I turn to tell you once more: pray, pray!

I bless the entire Holy Church. I bless in a special way the local church of Amazonas. I bless all the missionaries of My Son Jesus. It is necessary to evangelize for there are many hearts that are still closed to God. The word of God must reach out to the most remote places because the word of God means life to all My children.

Priests, priests, priests be faithful to God. Priests, so dear to My heart, love God. Be united to Him. Bring His love to all the faithful. I invite you to be saints. Do not be a cause of sorrow for My Heart.

My beloved children who are present here today, pray with me again for the priests…

Our Lady prayed one Our Father and one "Glory Be" for the priests.

The one who is united to God shall fear nothing. Behold that the world will be renewed and a new dawn of peace will arrive. The battle between good and evil is coming to an end. I want you united to me in the day of My triumph, at the triumph of My Immaculate Heart. Whoever consecrates himself or herself to Me, I will be his/her intercessor before My Son Jesus. I bless you again: in the name of the Father, the Son, and the Holy Spirit. Amen!

I wait for you at Itapiranga, because that is the place chosen by my Immaculate Heart for the entire people of Amazonas. With the zeal of your love and your dedication build the Sanctuary of God here in the Amazonas. Be zealous for the work of God. Itapiranga is the source of grace and love of God for all my children. From Itapiranga the Lord shines His light to the whole world.

Itapiranga, Itapiranga, a place so simples and hidden, but so huge to the eyes of God. I thank you again for your presence, My children. Remain with God´s peace, in the name of the Father, the Son and the Holy Spirit. Amen!

January 23, 2001

Pray with Me for the Families

Whoever loves and serves the Lord is always heard in his prayers. The Lord always hears and responds to the ones who yearn for His love. Pray with Me for all the families…

The Virgin prayed three "Glory Be's" for the families.

Dear children, continue to love the Lord and to offer Him your love. I come from heaven to bless you as your Mother.

My Son Jesus sends Me here to grant you His blessings and grace. Pray with love! Pray each time more, so that the grace of God comes down from Heaven ever more.

This will be the year of great changes for the entire humanity. Be prepared! The Lord is returning once more upon the earth to gather His people together. The ones who belong to the Lord shall fear nothing.

I bless you with My Maternal blessing, a Mother´s blessing: in the name of the Father, the Son, and the Holy Spirit. Amen! Remain with the peace of Jesus!

January 25, 2001
St. Michael the Archangel:

I am the Archangel St. Michael!

Jesus and the Virgin have sent me here. I am St. Michael the Archangel!

The Queen of Peace is being sent to the entire world to invite Her children to conversion, but there are still many who do not heed Her messages or believe in her apparitions.

Pray truly with your hearts. Open your hearts to God. The Queen of Peace is demanding obedience from each one of you. Whoever does not obey will suffer greatly yet, for the ones who do not listen to the voice from Heaven do not please God. If you are obedient you will find salvation. The Mother of God blesses you, together with Her Son Jesus, Our Lord. I bless you in His name and in the name of the Holy Trinity: in the name of the Father, the Son and the Holy Spirit. Amen!

January 30, 2001

Pray for the Holy Spirit

Peace be with you!

Dear children, I am your celestial Mother and I love you.

I want to tell you tonight that God loves you and blesses you, bestowing upon you many blessings. Open up your hearts to Him and receive His message of love. If you do this, peace will enter your hearts, remain with you, and it will come to your families.

Pray to the Holy Spirit. He will guide you, showing you the way of the truth, and your mission. I love you, and as a mother I desire to help you fulfill God's will. Pray always, because within your prayers God will reveal Himself, as well as His love. I bless you all: in the name of the Father, the Son, and the Holy Spirit. Amen!

The Virgin issued a message to a person:

Tell my son not to worry. I love him the way he is and I know his capabilities. If he opens himself to love he may comprehend what I desire from him. What I desire is that whatever he does he does with love, even if he is not able of doing everything, that all his intentions be based on love. It is God who sanctifies and perfects everything. Let God lead everything.

January 31, 2001
Conversion is to Live a New Life with God

Dear children, I am the Mother of Jesus, and tonight I wish to thank you for your prayers. The Lord blesses you and invites you to conversion. Do you know what conversion means? Conversion is to live a new life with God, totally renewed, freed from all evil and from every sinful attitude. Conversion is to live a life with love and forgiveness with each other, truly loving each other in Jesus, My Beloved Son. Conversion is to live a life of respect towards your brethren, for everyone is a temple of the Holy Spirit and a precious part of Him.

For that reason, My dear children, bear a great love and respect for all My children, hence you shall make God and Myself happy. Pray always more and your lives will be renewed by the Love of God. I bless you all: in the name of the Father, the Son, and the Holy Spirit. Amen!

January 31, 2001
St. Joseph:

The priest must respect the works of God

My dear son, peace be with you and with everyone.

Today, I pour upon all humanity the graces from my Most Chaste Heart. God wishes that all mankind benefits from His grace, through the intercession of My Heart to Him.

I love humankind and I desire that it comes closer to Me, because I wish to help humanity to walk always towards heaven, to God.

You are to tell your bishop to see to it well, pondering with love and discernment what Jesus and the Most Holy Virgin, My spouse, have done at Itapiranga.

Itapiranga is a great grace and a gift from God for the people of Amazonas and for the entire humanity. Itapiranga must be better known by the children of God, for the message that was transmitted there will be for the salvation of many souls.

The priests must know how to respect the works of God. How saddened God becomes when the priests, without knowing about the messages and apparition, criticize them and ridicule them. Those are worse than the scribes and Pharisees. Those are the "Thomas" of our days.

Priests, the Lord calls you to a deep reflection on your attitudes. Be careful and zealous for the work of the Lord, because what He does is for the salvation of your people, the same ones left aside, and abandoned by many of you, who with a bad example, did not fulfill your vocation and ministry as one should.

Pray to the Holy Spirit, He will help you to be faithful to your vocation. Ask for My aid and I will come to assist you. I bless all of you: in the name of the Father, the Son and the Holy Spirit. Amen!

February 2, 2001

Pray, Pray, Pray and You Shall Become the Most Beautiful Flowers in the Garden of God

Peace be with you!

Dear children, convert yourselves and live a holy and prayerful life.

The Lord once more calls you, through Me, to a change in your lives. Be faithful to your Christian commitments as spouses, children, brothers and sisters, and as parents. Do not allow Satan to destroy your families and the peace God granted them through His presence.

Many times when I see that you do not listen to me, I become concerned. My words are not a joke. Take a concrete decision to convert because your time is running out. Woe to those who do not heed my messages and my apparitions and waste the grace from Heaven. I pray for your conversion and so you decide for the path that leads to God.

I bless all My ill children, and I pray asking the blessing of God and His grace over all of them. Pray, pray, pray and you shall become the most beautiful flowers in the garden of God, watered by His Holy Love. I bless you all: in the name of the Father, the Son, and the Holy Spirit. Amen!

May 13, 2001
Lady of the Rosary and Mother of All
Humanity

Peace be with you!

Dear children, I am the Lady of the Rosary and Mother of all humanity.

Pray the Rosary. Your prayers are still important for the salvation of many souls. Do penance. Many do not offer sacrifice for the salvation of their brethren. I invite you again: fast. Do not disregard fasting. It will be very important, My children. Pay attention to what I tell you.

The Creator allowed me to speak to you again. Be obedient to God. Ask for God's mercy every day for this world, for Brazil and for the Amazonas.

Amazonas! Amazonas! How much sufferings I foresee if you do not heed my appeal!

Again, I warn My favorite sons. Why do you not listen to Me? Why do you not heed My appeals, My favorite little children, priests of my Immaculate Heart? Do you not love your mother? I love you very much, and for that reason I am here to help you, My priest sons.

I came to Amazonas to aid all of My children: bishops, priests, consecrated ones, the faithful, and all those who need My Maternal help. I did not come down from Heaven for fun, but for a very serious reason: to invite you to love, peace, unity and obedience to the Commandments of God, and to His Holy Church.

At this moment, I pour down from Heaven a shower of blessings. The Creator at this moment looks at each one of you and blesses you. Turn your crosses and sorrows into blessings for the salvation of many souls, offering them up to God so that He will sanctify them. Do not be afraid. Do not have fear in the face of tribulations. God is with you.

From here I bless My favorite son, the Holy Father, the pope. Today the whole world is united in continuous and fervent prayer. Many of My children are praying in Fatima. Today Francisco and Jacinta are by My side, blessing you and praying for you to God. They have suffered and were courageous, never renounced their faith and their love to this Mother who loves humankind.

My children, there are too many sins and offenses against God. Poor sinful humankind! But you can help her if you pray, sacrificing yourselves offering God reparations and sacrifices for the conversion of sous, as my 3 little shepherds did.

Behold, the Lord will renew everything. The world will be renewed and the love of God shall reign in every heart, in the life of all of My children. Blessed are those who open their hearts to God. The Lord has prepared many blessings for those who listen to and live His Word. Remain with the peace of God, take it to every man and woman, for the world will be renewed so that every man and woman may live as true brothers and sisters.

I am the star who precedes the second coming of the Lord. I am the One who shall crush the head of the serpent. I am your Mother and the Queen of Heaven and of earth. For all of you My maternal love and blessing: in the name of the Father, the Son, and of the Holy Spirit. Amen!

June 23, 2001

Feast of the Immaculate Heart of Mary

I saw the Most Holy Virgin at the Our Lady of Remedies Church, in Manaus. She was so beautiful. This apparition took place during communion, after I received communion. The Virgin appeared in front of the altar, when Father James was distributing communion to the faithful. She was a little over him, in the air. Her mantle was large, and there were two angels holding it behind the Virgin. It was silvery white, and in its inner side it was blue. Her tunic was white, in the same style of the mantle. She was showing Her Immaculate Heart which was of a very bright red color, as I had never seen before, and from it emanated intense rays of light over everyone in the church. I also understood that those rays were designated for the whole world.

On the Virgin's head there was a crown of white roses. She was very happy and she told me:

> *The Lord has sent me here so that the humankind will be benefitted by His grace, through My Immaculate Heart and My maternal blessing.*
>
> *Today the world and the Church are receiving My blessings and grace that comes from the Lord and are transmitted through the rays of light that depart from My maternal heart.*

Looking at Father James, the Virgin approached him delicately and put her right hand over him. She inclined her head and as a sign of respect to Jesus in the Eucharist and to the priest who was distributing the hosts to the faithful, for he is a minister of God. The Virgin cheerfully asked me to tell the priest:

Tell My favorite son that My Immaculate Heart is joyful and I am thankful for the procession he permitted in honor of this heart of mine, pure and virginal, that God has granted Me, enriching it with His love, grace and blessings, being his vase of virtues, of grace and protection to those who approach Him with Love, devotion and respect. The Lord God, rich in love and mercy, and desirous to grant salvation to the souls, aiding them by a simple gesture of love done to His Most Holy Mother, showing Himself generous and prone to distribute His gifts and grace ever more to all His children.

It was at this moment that the Mother of God, slowly moving down from above, touched the church's floor with her feet, where the priest had distributed the hosts, right at the center. Since the beginning of the apparition, I have realized that the Virgin did not have the cloud that was always beneath her feet, and so I understood the reason for her act. She remained silent for a moment, looking at me and at everyone in the church. I said to myself:

"Forgive me Mother for not kneeling, if I do that I will attract everyone's attention, and they may notice that something is taking place. For that reason I remained seated!"

She smiled as if listening to me. Afterwards I thought to myself:

"How I wish I could go where You are and kiss your feet that are now touching this floor, and also kiss the place where you are stepping on, for it seems so unclean for her holy, beautiful and perfect feet to tread on!"

She smiled at me even more and said:

Every spot in the house of God is holy and worthy of respect. For God everything is clean and perfect, for wherever God is, everything is sanctified by His presence.

Real dirt only enters His house, His Holy Temple, when men come to Church with their rotten souls, decayed by the most horrible sins, and go many times toward the holy altar of the Lord, offending Him with the most horrible transgressions and sacrileges committed against Him in the Holy Eucharist. This is the only way that filthiness enters the House of God.

Afterwards she extended her hands over the assembly, as if she were praying for her children in silence. Then, lowering her hands, she looked at me again, saying:

It is here, in this most sublime moment, of the union of God with the souls, during the Eucharist, that many miracles take place and many hearts are renewed through His love. This is the moment in which the Lord heals many people from spiritual blindness, from their cold and hardened hearts, granting them many spiritual blessings, as well as many physical blessings for their infirmities.

I am the Queen of all hearts, I desire to have all the hearts warmed here, inside My Immaculate Heart, through the flames of My love, so that those hearts will ever be more on fire to have a greater and more profound love for the Lord.

I saw many small hearts entering the heart of Our Lady and becoming beautiful, radiant, with a similar vivid color as that of her Immaculate Heart. The Virgin continued:

Here in this place where I have appeared, the Lord wishes to heal many souls with His Love, offering to all My children the remedy to all their infirmities, through the Eucharist that was worthily and saintly received, and through the graces that flow from My Immaculate Heart, that your Celestial Mother deigned to reveal so lovingly and maternally to all her children and as a strong and efficacious means to obtain the blessings from God. To all of you My maternal blessing, from the bottom of my Heart: in the name of the Father, the Son, and the Holy Spirit. Amen!

I also saw the Most Chaste Heart of St. Joseph, above the Virgin, very luminous and beautiful, surrounded by white lilies. I understood that the Virgin, during the feast of her Immaculate Heart, was requesting that the Church recognizes the feast day to honor St. Joseph's heart and devotion to him.

June 27, 2001
Feast of the Most Chaste Heart of St. Joseph

St. Joseph's Message

Dear son, God has assigned to you a great mission: to transmit the devotion to my Most Chaste Heart to the world. What an honorable, beautiful and wonderful mission!

Amongst so many people, I have chosen you, even in the past, when you were away from the Lord, when you were not His yet and you followed your own paths. But I asked the Lord that He would look down upon the one I had chosen in Amazonas, as His family.

Do you know why I wished to appear in a home to reveal My heart to the world? Because I wish to show the world how much I love the families and how much they are important to God, for I was the chief of the Holy Family and I still am.

The Lord has granted me a great glory. He gave Me the grace of having a chaste and virginal heart. He created a holy heart for me, where He could place His grace.

Truly, my Most Chaste Heart is full of the most abundant blessings from the Lord, filled with virtues and blessings.

I am the righteous one of the Lord. He who has always grown in divine virtues, and in the grace of God. Those who call upon My holy name, the most worthy and holy name that the Lord has dedicated to Me, and called Me by, I promise the abundance of my celestial blessings, and My protection against all the iniquities from hell, and the immediate deliverance, in all dangers and afflictions.

You saw today how much I love you and wish your wellbeing. Today many have witnessed the protection I grant you. Fear Nothing. The enemy cannot harm you, for I accompany you.

Today, through your prayers and the prayers of your brothers and sisters, much illness that the Enemy wished to unleash against the church of Amazonas and the souls were destroyed. Whatever he had planned will not take place and the grace of God will come down upon you and your families.

My heart will shine ever more in the world.

At that moment I saw in many parts of the world people doing processions, great celebration and works in honor of the Most Chaste Heart of St. Joseph. Right then I saw the globe representing the world. In it, small lights started to appear on each continent, shining in many places until there were many lights shining intensely in many places. I heard the voice of St. Joseph saying:

It shall be that way!

I understood that where the lights were glowing those would be the places where the heart of St. Joseph would be honored, and where his devotion would reach. As I saw in my vision, it will reach every place in the world. St. Joseph continued, saying:

> *Hence my children may benefit from the grace of God. I thank you for your presence and for the love you have offered to me. To all of you my paternal blessing and protection: in the name of the Father, the Son and the Holy Spirit. Amen!*

July 7, 2001
Assisi, Italy

The Littlest Ones are Those Who Can Receive Everything from His Merciful Heart

Today God blesses you. God makes Himself present in the union of one with another. He fulfills His work as He pleases and takes it forward. He never abandons His people, His children, those who serve Him with an open heart, and trust Him.

The littlest ones are those who can receive everything from His merciful heart. The little ones include all those who are humble, who have no pretensions, those who dedicate themselves confidently to His loving plan, who do not doubt His kindness and never allow pride and conceit to approach their hearts. It means those who, in their nothingness, allow God to do everything.

I love you like a mother and I offer you My aid, for God has allowed Me to favor you. Bring the work of God forward, do not get discouraged. I thank you for your disposition My child. You will always go ahead, taking my messages and fulfilling the Lord's will. You shall still visit other *places, like Francisco* did. I bless all of you: in the name of the Father, of the Son, and of the Holy Spirit. Amen!*

*St. Francis of Assisi

July 8, 2001

I Love You and I Bring You to My Immaculate Heart

My dear children, I love you and I place you in My Immaculate Heart. Pray, because with prayer your hearts will be filled with God`s love and He will bring you peace. Jesus loves you. I give you today His peace, a peace that He allows Me to grant you, because I Am the Queen of Peace.

Belong to Jesus and give testimony of the love of God to your brothers and sisters- by doing so you will help God's kingdom expand to the whole world and in their lives.

The Lord is happy for your presence and prayers. As your mother I bless you: in the name of the Father, of the Son, and of the Holy Spirit. Amen!

July 9, 2001

Do Not Reject the Gift That Was Given to You

Beloved son, I wish to give you My message...that came as a great grace to My Church, because it has emerged from the deep mysteries of My Heart, which were concealed in My secret, and now it is revealed ever more to the Church.

Do not worry about what you are to say. It is I who will speak. You must only write my message. Give thanks to the Father for everything that you have learned and heard from My mouth, for He desires everyone to be dressed by the Spirit of Truth.

The Holy Trinity is with you and everyone. Today I address you. Do you understand all that is currently happening? Those are great things My son. You have not evaluated these events yet, but you will understand My plans ever more.

Edson, you were called by Me. Again I tell you, as I said at the beginning of your journey: (*) do not reject the gift that was given you, the grace I have granted you, when the elderly assembly put their hands over you, receiving you as a prophecy. Do you remember that moment?

I was then preparing you for everything that is happening now. Be faithful. Do not be afraid!

All I want is confidence, for only thus I may use you for My work, in My way. Courage. Take heart. Forward. It is time to leave the deep sleep, to be awake and attentive when the Lord comes and calls you to follow Him. I bless all of you: in the name of the Father, of the Son, and the Holy Spirit. Amen!

* 1 Timothy 4, 14-15

July 11, 2001
Palermo, Italy

Be Builders of Peace

Peace be with you!

My beloved children, I am Jesus' Mother and the Queen of Peace. Today I bless you and pour My love upon you. I never abandon you. God sent Me here to invite you to live in peace and in love among yourselves.

Be builders of peace. Help those most in need. Be an example of love and truth. If you do not love your brethren and do not give you help to your neighbors, you will not be doing anything. Do not allow selfishness and self-indulgence to take over your hearts. Give yourself totally for the happiness of your most suffering brothers.

I carry you in My Immaculate Heart. Here in My Heart you will receive many graces from the Lord. I am happy for your presence and for your prayers.

Today I am also blessing your families. Be faithful to God. Be obedient to the Church. Be true apostles of My Son Jesus. I bless My favorite children. I bless all of you: in the name of the Father, of the Son, and the Holy Spirit. Amen!

July 12, 2001

Be the Children of God, not Children of the Darkness

Peace be with you!

Dear children, I am the Queen of Peace. I invite you to prayer and conversion. Pray, pray and pray. Through prayer you will find peace and joy from God and thus your lives will be transformed. As your Mother I bless you and I place you inside My Heart.

My dear youth, thank you for your presence. Today I bless you in a special manner and I present you to Jesus. You are important to God. In order for you to understand My call: pray! Do not let the goodness in you be destroyed by sin. Be the children of God, not children of darkness. Each one of you is special to My Heart. If you dedicate your hearts to Me I can offer them to Jesus. Pray for your families and for the youth of the whole world.

If you pray, many will find God's light and will be saved. May prayer be always part of your life. Jesus has sent me here to grant you His grace and His love.

Do not fear anything because God is always with you and protects you. If you heed My plea you will be concurring to the good and the peace of this world.

Listen to Me! Listen to Me! Listen to Me! I speak to you as a loving and kind mother, because all of you are My children. I send you My kiss of love and My blessing: in the name of the Father, of the Son, and of the Holy Spirit. Amen.

July 13, 2001

Those Who Pray for the Priests
Have the Blessing of God

Peace be with you!

My children, continue to follow the path designed by God. God loves you so, and His great love encompasses you at this moment.

The Lord sends His light and blessing from heaven. May each one of you who are here be true witness of love. Amen, amen, amen. Love transforms and sanctifies you. With love, everything that does not bring you peace will be destroyed. When you love, you are always more united to God, who is true love.

Thank you for your presence. Tomorrow I will return with My Son Jesus Who will come to bless you. Pray for the Church and for My sons, the priests. Those who pray for the priests have God's blessing. I bless all of you: in the name of the Father, of the Son, and the Holy Spirit. Amen!

July 14, 2001

I am the Queen of Heaven and Earth and your Mother

Peace be with you!

Dear children, I am the Queen of Heaven and Earth, and your Mother.

Today I bless you, together with My son Jesus, Who is here at My side.

Jesus loves you so and desires from you obedience and humility. Be humble and simple, in order for you to deserve the kingdom of Heaven. Do not fear anything, for I am here to protect you and place you under my Immaculate mantle.

Be children of prayer and faith. Increase your faith by daily asking God for it in your prayers. I thank you for your presence and for the love you have for Me and for My Son Jesus. I bless all of you: in the name of the Father, of the Son, and the Holy Spirit. Amen!

July 15, 2001

I am Happy for Your Presence

Peace be with you!

Dear children, I am happy for your presence. I love you so and desire your salvation. Continue to pray the holy Rosary. Know that your prayers are helping Me to establish My plans of conversion.

Today I grant you all my love, so that you may transmit it to all My children.

Strive for the construction of God's kingdom on earth, so that you may one day deserve the Kingdom of heaven. Heaven waits for you!

Each time more God's work is being fulfilled. In Heaven, you shall receive a great reward from God. Do not be discouraged.

Be truthful, obedient, and humble, because humility pleases My Maternal Heart.

Give thanks to God for everything that He is doing. I bless you and keep you within My heart. I bless all of you: in the name of the Father, of the Son, and the Holy Spirit. Amen!

July 16, 2001

Seek to Understand the Signs
of the End of the Times

Peace be with you!

Dear children, once more the Creator sends Me here to grant you His divine blessings. God is presently granting abundant graces to the world. Open your hearts My children and try to understand the signs of the end of the times. This is a time of special blessings. God is calling you every day to conversion either through a small sign from nature or through your neighbor. He never forsakes you. In fact, many people neglect God, rejecting His call, disobeying and rebelling against Him.

As your Mother, dear children, I ask you this: be obedient to God, listen to His calling! A soul that do not live by obedience will never become saint, because it distances itself ever more from the path of sainthood.

If you live by obedience, God will enrich you with His blessings and may sanctify you.

I bless in a special way all My children who are ill and going through great hardships. Take heart. I am here to assist you. Offer your suffering to Me, so that I may comfort you and be your intercessor before God, My beloved Son Jesus Christ. Pray, pray, pray and God shall grant you His grace and blessings.

Thank you for your presence. Thank you for your willingness to be here

*to listen to my message. Thank for your love devoted to
Me and to My Son Jesus. Do not forget My Most Chaste
Spouse Joseph. I bless all of you: in the name of the Father,
of the Son, and the Holy Spirit. Amen!*

July 16, 2001

Vision of the Holy Family

I was in the city of Sciacca, in the province of Agrigento,
Sicily, Italy, visiting a local youth group. In the afternoon,
after praying the Rosary and giving my testimony at the
church of Our Lady of Rosary of Fatima, which is run by the
Capuchin Friars, I had a vision of the Holy Family, in front of
the people who were there.

Have a Scapular Made

In this apparition, Our Lady gave me a message and said:

*Pay attention to what I will show you. Have a scapular
made according to what you shall see. That will be the
scapular of St. Joseph. My Son Jesus and I wish everyone
to wear it with love and faith, in deep honor to my spouse
Joseph, as He deserves. Those who bear this scapular shall
receive the protection from God, through the Most Chaste
Heart and his sheltering mantle, as well as many blessings
necessary for their salvation and sainthood.*

*Over the image of the Holy Family, I saw the following phrase written in golden letters: "**Most Chaste Heart of St. Joseph**" and bellow: "**Be the guardian of our family!**"*

Soon afterwards, this vision disappeared, to give place to three illumined and glowing hearts. There were two rays of light coming from the Heart of Jesus and going towards the Immaculate Heart of Mary and to the Most Chaste Heart of St. Joseph, and from them, the rays departed and were directed to the world. Above those Hearts, these words appeared, written in golden letters: **"Jesus, Mary and Joseph,"** and under them: "**I love Thee, save souls!**"

Following this vision, Our Lady reappeared with Her Child Jesus and St. Joseph. Together, they blessed every one present and disappeared amidst the beautiful light that surrounded them. I did not know that on this day the Carmelite order and the Church around the world celebrated the 750th year in which Our Lady entrusted the scapular to St. Simon Stock. This was a very special day for the Carmelites, a grandiose event for the order of the Carmelites, and the day in which Jesus and Our Lady asked the Church and the world for the scapular of St. Joseph, as a special protection for the families of the whole world.

July 17, 2001

The World Needs Conversion

Peace be with you!

Dear children, I am the Blessed Virgen Mary, Mother of Jesus.

Pray the holy Rosary every day, and thus God´s blessings will be poured down upon you and your family. I love you so much and I am here because I wish to grant you My Maternal Love.

The world needs to convert: I say it again! How many souls risk being eternally lost. Help Me, My little ones, help Me with your prayers, so that the world may find the light of God and convert.

I am always at your side and never abandon you. Thank you for the prayers that you have offered to God and to Me for the salvation of souls. Do penances and sacrifices always for the salvation of souls. I bless all of you: in the name of the Father, of the Son, and the Holy Spirit. Amen!

July 20, 2001

May Your Hearts be Always Focused on Heaven

Peace be with you!

Dear children, I am your Mother and I love you so much. Abundant goodness I desire for you and your families. My Immaculate Heart is joyful, because your prayers are helping Me to save many souls.

Always pray the holy Rosary. If you offer Me your prayers with love and devotion, then I can intercede with my Son Jesus, so that they will be transformed into blessings and graces for you, for your families and for the whole world.

Jesus always waits for you in the Tabernacle and in the church. He loves you very much and desires your salvation. He, the Omnipotent and Holy one, the one Who is, Who was, and is to come, shall renew the entire world with the blazing fire of love that comes from His Sacred Heart.

How many wonders My Son Jesus is performing in the world! My little children, do not ever think that My apparitions in this world are of little importance, because if they did not happen, as they do now, many souls would have already been eternally suffering in hell – but because of My apparitions, they have found light and divine grace and were saved, for they have lived according to My appeals.

When I appeared to My little Portuguese shepherds at Fatima, I taught them this little prayer:

Oh My Jesus, forgive our sins, save us from the fires of hell, lead all souls to Heaven , and help especially those in most need of your mercy.

Why have I taught them this prayer? Because I desire the salvation of all the souls and I wish to teach My children how to ask Jesus for their salvation and for the salvation of their brethren. I want also to reveal to them the existence of hell – to where the souls of sinners who refuse to convert go. However, through prayer, everything can change, since God is attentive to the intercessory prayers for those who are far from the path that leads to Him. I also want to reveal the existence of purgatory to everyone, where the souls suffer and wait for the final moment of their purification, so that they can be eternally united to the Lord in Heaven.

May your hearts be always focused on Heaven and not on the things of this world. Everything will pass away, My children, only God remains. Appertain totally to Jesus, I tell you again. Thank you for your prayers and your presence. I bless all of you: in the name of the Father, of the Son, and the Holy Spirit. Amen!

July 26, 2001

Each Person in Here has a Mission to Accomplish

Peace be with you!

Dear children, I am the Queen of Peace and the Mother of Jesus. I am very happy today with your presence and with the presence of My sons priests.

I call you once more to conversion and prayer. Be with Jesus. Love Jesus. Again I tell you to persevere in your journey towards God, for He never abandons you and is always at your side.

Everyone here has a mission to accomplish. I have not gathered you here for nothing, but to help you to comprehend more and more the mission that God has reserved for you. My little children, I call you to pray more to the Holy Spirit, asking Him for the knowledge and true discernment of your mission.

I have noble things to tell you, and the Almighty invites you to live a holier life, through Me.

Each day, more and more, My work of salvation and conversion, entrusted to Me by My Son Jesus, is taking place, through My apparitions in the world.

Itapiranga, Itapiranga, sanctuary of grace and blessings that God has prepared for the young people of the whole world and for all families.

Pray for peace in the hearts on My children. Many do not have peace in their lives, because they are far from God. If you pray, abundant love and peace will come down to the world.

I bless all of you: in the name of the Father, of the Son, and the Holy Spirit. Amen!

July 28, 2001

Each Word from my Messages is like a Loving Heartbeat from my Immaculate Heart

Peace be with you!

Dear children, I love you very much and I always wish to lead you to My Son Jesus.

My Maternal love pushes Me to come here again, to this place, chosen and blessed by the Lord, to invite you to live a holier life.

Be always united in prayers, as an act of worship and gratitude to the Lord, Who continues to perform His wonders in the world.

My little children, you shall always come closer to Jesus in the Eucharist. Only He is the life for your souls, and your strength during times of trials.

Pray and sacrifice yourselves for those who do not believe in God and do not love Him. Know that your prayers are very precious in the eyes of God. You are helping your brethren, who are far from the path of salvation, to return to it with a contrite heart.

Do not fear anything! Your celestial Mother is always accompanying you with a Maternal care. I will help you to be faithful to God if you let yourselves be guided by Me and open up your hearts.

Each word from My messages is like a loving heartbeat from my Immaculate Heart. Every beat of my Heart is a call to a soul. When you are united and praying, you find strength to walk with faith in this faithless world.

Amen, glorify and truthfully worship the Lord of Heaven and earth, and your lives shall be transformed.

It is time for you to deliver ever more My messages to the youth. I send you today to your brothers and sisters, so that you may deliver to them My Maternal plea and love.

Dear young people, thank you for your disposition and contribution to this plan of love from My Lord.

Ask for wisdom from the Omnipotent and He shall grant it to you; so that you will know what to do, how to speak and how to act. Courage. Courage. Now, many are ready to do something for their brethren. This is the moment to show everyone the light of God that shines within you. To all of you, I give my blessing once more: in the name of the Father, the Son and the Holy Spirit. Amen!

July 29, 2001

My Mother is Tireless

May My peace be with all of you!

My little children, I'm Jesus, the Son of the Eternal Father and of the Blessed Virgin Mary. I love you all and I wish to have you in My arms. My embrace is strong and I wish to protect you against all evil.

My hands are always extended towards you because I desire to bless you. How glad am I to see your response of love to Me and to My heavenly Mother.

My Mother is the Queen of peace, because She is united with Me in heaven for all eternity. From Heaven She prays for you, pleading before My throne for the necessary graces for all of you.

My mother is tireless. She wishes happiness for all of you. Today She asked me to come to bless you, that is why I Am here.

She is the Queen of Heaven and earth, of all Angels and Saints in paradise. In Her humility, meekness and silence, the great mystery of human salvation has begun, through My coming to this world and, once again, I wish to grant you the grace of salvation through Her Immaculate heart.

Come to My Immaculate Mother, so that holiness will come faster into your lives. Her Most Blessed Name (Mary) is a powerful shield against all evil and danger, just as the Most Holy Name of My father Joseph.

Always invoke these two Most Holy Names, united to My Sacred Name, then graces and blessings from heaven will come down upon you and your family.

I am always with you, by your side, My little ones, and today I place in your little hearts some of My divine love so that you may learn how to love and to serve.

What a deep mystery it is to know how to love and to serve, donating yourself to your neighbor and to the one most in need. When you lay down your life to your brethren, your souls are purified and set free from faults and worldly attachments, and so you are more united to Me and to Heaven.

Wherever your brethren are, there I also am. I always wait for you in your brethren, to grant you My love and My blessings. When you love those who do not love you, you become more and more like me.

Amen, Amen, Amen. Now I bless you with a special blessing. May you be witnesses of My presence and my appeals to all your brethren. I bless you all In the name of the Father, and of the Son, and of the Holy Spirit. Amen.

Early September

Our Lady Appeared to my Mother very Sorrowful

Pray, Maria do Carmo, otherwise many will die. Pray, my daughter, help Me with your prayers and pray much for God's mercy for the world.

My mother heard the voice of several people screaming and crying in distress.

September 11, 2001

Terrorist Attack in the United States of America

Our Lady appeared, crying. Thick tears rolled down Her face. She did not give any message. She covered Her face with Her hands and cried, disappearing right after. Who can understand the pain She felt in Her heart and the sadness in Her face for what had happened? Let us console Our Holy Mother by changing our lives, and abandoning the path of sin that each day makes other victims.

September 12, 2001

Our Lady is very sad these days. She asks for prayers for the world and for peace. Let us pray to help Her fulfill Her plan of conversion and salvation of humanity. Each prayer is precious and a source of life and grace to the world, and light to the hardened and gloomy hearts.

November 14, 2001

I am Our Lady of the Immaculate Conception!

My peace to you and your family, Maria do Carmo. I am Our Lady of the Immaculate Conception!

I come from heaven to beg the people of Amazonas to pray more so that they may be preserved from suffering the consequences of the war. Make a one-hour vigil every day. Remain daily in prayer. Go to adoration to the Holy Sacrament after the Mass, at least ten minutes a day, asking for the end of the war in the whole world. This is the request of a very much afflicted and concerned Mother. Thank you for responding to My call. May My peace and the peace of My Son be with you: In the name of the Father, and of the Son, and of the Holy Spirit. Amen!

The Holy Virgin left this message to my mother after the terrorist attacks on September 11th. Two days before this attack she had appeared and told her to pray much asking God to be merciful to the world, because something very sad and terrible would strike humanity. The Virgin delivered this message to My mother with a painful heart. For that reason, She asked for prayers on the intention of the end of the war and asking for divine protection because new armed conflicts had begun, which could reach other countries if prayers and reparation were not offered to God.

When the Virgin asked for the ten minutes daily adoration, She meant to show us that many do not devote not even five minutes to the Holy Sacrament. She asked for at least ten minutes because it is good to be in adoration for an extended time. However, many have not yet opened their hearts to this request, living it deeply. When chastisement comes to the world, many will desire to adore Jesus, to beg Him for strength, to be with Him in the Most Holy Sacrament, but they will not be able to, because there might not be enough time left. And God will show them that they could have done that before, in peace and tranquility, but they did not want to, by despising and losing the opportunity and the grace to adore Him in the churches, in the Most Blessed Sacrament.

December 30, 2001
Feast of the Holy Family

> *Be a light to this world that does not live peace. Pray that goodness subdue evil in your families.*

DOCUMENTS OF OFFICIAL ECCLESIASTICAL APPROVAL OF ITAPIRANGA

(English Translations are followed by the original documents)

English Translation:

BY THE GRACE OF GOD AND DESIGNATION OF THE APOSTOLIC SEE

BISHOP OF ITACOATIARA

ORDER OF WORSHIP

Since 1994 many Catholics make pilgrimages to Itapiranga in a place called "Sanctuary" to venerate Virgin Mary. These pilgrimages resulted and are still resulting in many graces. Without falling into sensationalism and fanaticism they are developing a spirit of prayer and renewal, and reinforcing the pilgrims faith within God's people.

After studying carefully the events, I authorize these pilgrimages and the public cult to be celebrated in the chapel, or in the area known as the cross to invoke Our Lady under the title of Queen of the Rosary and Peace. All the manifestations of public cult such as the Holy Mass and confessions, will be under the responsibility of the priest for which he was indicated.

This Order of Worship seeks to promote the spiritual life of God's people arriving here to honor the apparitions of Our Lady which originated the devotion to this place.

Anyway, after the first evaluation done by a group of people chosen by me, starting this year, a Committee chosen and established by me, will continue to accompany and analyze the facts and events that happened and continue to happen here, gathering all the necessary medical and theological information, as well as witnesses and objective elements for a first judgment about the events that occurred in Itapiranga and this way give the church a sure and credible base.

31 January 2010
Dom Carillo Gritti
Bishop Prelate

POR GRAÇA DE DEUS E DESIGNAÇÃO DA SÉ APOSTÓLICA

BISPO DE ITACOATIARA

DECRETO DE CULTO

Desde 1994, muitos católicos fazem peregrinações para Itapiranga, num lugar chamado "Santuário" para venerar a Virgem Maria. Estas peregrinações e romarias deram e estão dando muitos frutos de graça. Sem cair na tentação de sensacionalismo e do fanatismo, elas estão desenvolvendo no meio do povo de Deus um espírito de oração e renovando e reforçando a fé dos peregrinos.

Depois de ter estudado com atenção os acontecimentos, autorizo estas peregrinações e o culto público, celebrado na capela ou no lugar do cruzeiro para invocar Nossa Senhora sob o título de Rainha do Rosário e da Paz. Toda a manifestação de culto público, como a Santa Missa, Confissões será sob a responsabilidade pastoral do sacerdote para isso indicado.

Este Decreto de Culto, visa favorecer a vida espiritual do povo de Deus que aqui chega para honrar as aparições de Nossa Senhora que deram origem a esta devoção neste lugar.

Enfim, depois de um primeiro discernimento feito por um grupo de pessoas por mim escolhidas, a partir deste ano, uma Comissão escolhida e instituída por mim, vai continuar acompanhando e analisando os fatos e eventos que aqui aconteceram e ainda acontecem, recolhendo toda a informação médica e teológica necessárias, além dos testemunhos e elementos objetivos finais para um justo e reto juízo sobre os eventos ocorridos em Itapiranga e assim oferecer uma base segura e credível à Igreja.

Itacoatiara, 31 de janeiro de 2010

Dom Carillo Gritti

Bispo Prelado

English Translation:

Dom Carillo Gritti
Bishop Prelate

Itapiranga (Amazonas) on the 02 of May 1994 Our Lady manifested Herself to Edson Glauber Coutinho.

A common young man with his studies completed, already forwarded to prayer within the family by his mother, to whom Our Lady first came speaking, but only seeing the boy.

These manifestations in which Our Lady liked to be called Queen of the Holy Rosary and of Peace, progressed in a way that the young Edson, first just seeing, then seeing and hearing, kept happening during 14 years and at the present time Our Lady only manifests Herself through messages.

The young man, who comes from a simple but not needy family with a heart of authentic attitude and prayer and a particular devotion to Our Lady, I introduce as "sincere and devout" bearer of visions and messages worthy of being appreciated. Actually, a Theological Committee named by me is analyzing the likely supernatural nature of the events and messages.

Being that on the various manifestations, the Virgin has called for a devotion to the Three Sacred Hearts of Jesus, Mary, and Joseph, on the 02 of May of 2010, we launched the first stone for a new Sanctuary in honor of the three Sacred Hearts in the certainty that one day it will be a place of many pilgrimages. The conversions that only God, by the intercession of Mary, can operate, have been for me, and the enlightened souls, enough and sufficient reason to see, in the visions and messages, God's finger. May God and Our Lady together with Her most chaste spouse St. Joseph, accompany us on this path of reevangelizaion in the land of Amazonas.

Dom Carillo Gritti
Bishop Prelate of Itacoatiara

DOM CARILLO GRITTI
BISPO PRELADO
RUA MONS. JOAQUIM PEREIRA, N° 144 — CENTRO
ITACOATIARA (AMAZONAS) BRASIL
EMAIL: DOMCARILLOGRITTI@GMAIL.COM

Itapiranga (Amazonas) 1994, 02/05, Nossa Senhora se manifesta a
EDSON GLAUBER COUTINHO.

Um jovem simples, curso completo nos estudos, já encaminhado à
oração na própria família pela mãe, a quem primeira se manifestou
Nossa Senhora falando e só vendo o jovem.

Nestas manifestações em que Nossa Senhora gostou chamar-se
Rainha do Santo Rosário e da Paz, foram progredindo de forma que o
jovem Edson, antes vendo, depois vendo e ouvindo, foram-se
repetindo ao longo de quatorze anos de forma que atualmente é só
por mensagens que se manifesta.

O jovem, que pertence a uma família simples, não necessitada, que
possue no coração autêntica atitude a oração e tem particular
devoção a Nossa Senhora, eu apresento como "sincero e devoto",
portador de visões e mensagens dignas de serem apreciadas. Com
efeito por uma Comissão Teológica instituída por mim, estamos
apreciando a provável natureza sobrenatural dos eventos e das
mensagens.

Sendo que, nas diversas manifestações a Virgem tem conclamado
para uma devoção aos Três Sagrados Corações de Jesus, Maria e
José, aos 02/05 deste ano 2010, lançamos a primeira pedra de um
novo Santuário em honra dos Três Sagrados Corações, na certeza
que seja um dia lugar de muitas peregrinações. As conversões, que
somente Deus pela intercessão de Maria pode operar, têm sido até
agora para mim e almas iluminadas, motivo bastante e suficiente
para ver nestas visões e mensagens o dedo de Deus.

Que Deus e Nossa Senhora, juntamente ao castíssimo Esposo dela
São José, nos acompanhem neste caminho de re-evangelização desta
terra do Amazonas.

+ _Carillo Gritti_

Dom Carillo Gritti
Bispo Prelado de Itacoatiara.

THE HOLY CLOAK
OF ST. JOSEPH

PRAYERS FOR THE NOVENA OF THE HOLY CLOAK

In the name of the Father, and of the Son, and of the Holy Spirit. Amen.

Jesus, Mary and Joseph, I give you my heart and my soul.

(Recite the Glory Be 3 times to our Heavenly Father in thanksgiving for having exalted St. Joseph to a position of such exceptional dignity.)

OFFERING

I

O Glorious Patriarch St. Joseph, I humbly prostrate myself before you. I beg the Lord Jesus, your Immaculate Spouse, the Blessed Virgin Mary, and all the Angels and Saints in the Heavenly Court, to join me in this devotion. I offer you this precious cloak, while pledging my sincerest faith and devotion.

I promise to do all in my power to honor you throughout my lifetime to prove my love for you.

Help me, St. Joseph. Assist me now and throughout my lifetime, but especially at the moment of my death, as you were assisted by Jesus and Mary, that I may join you one day in Heaven and there honor you for all eternity. Amen.

II

O Glorious Patriarch St. Joseph, prostrate, before you and your Divine Son, Jesus, I offer you, with heartfelt devotion, this precious treasury of prayers, being ever mindful of the numerous virtues which adorned your sacred person. In you, O Glorious Patriarch, was fulfilled the dream of your precursor the first Joseph, who indeed seemed to have been sent by God to prepare the way for your presence on this Earth. In fact, not only were you surrounded by the shining splendor of the rays of the Divine Sun, Jesus, but you were splendidly reflected in the brilliant light of the mystic moon, the Blessed Virgin Mary. O Glorious Patriarch, if the example of the ancient Jacob, who personally went to congratulate his favorite son, who was exalted on the throne of Egypt, served to bring all his progeny there, should not the example of Jesus and Mary, who honored you with their greatest respect and trust, serve to bring me, your devoted servant, to present you with this precious cloak in your honor.

Grant, O Great St. Joseph, that the Almighty God may turn a benevolent glance toward me. As the ancient Joseph did not reject his guilty and cruel brothers, but rather accepted them with love and protected and saved them from hunger and death, I beseech you, O Glorious Patriarch, through your intercession, grant that the Lord may never abandon me in this exiled valley of sorrows. Grant that He may always number me as one of your devoted servants who lives serenely under the patronage of your Holy Cloak. Grant that I may live always within the protection of this patronage, every day of my life and particularly at that moment when I draw my dying breath.

PRAYERS

I

Hail O Glorious St. Joseph, you who are entrusted with the priceless treasures of Heaven and Earth and foster-father of Him who nourishes all the creatures of the universe. You are, after Mary, the Saint most worthy of our love and devotion. You alone, above all the Saints, were chosen for that supreme honor of rearing, guiding, nourishing and even embracing the Messiah, whom so many kings and prophets would have so desired to behold.

St. Joseph, save my soul and obtain for me from the Divine Mercy of God that petition for which I humbly pray. And for the Holy Souls in Purgatory, grant a great comfort from their pain.

(Recite the Glory Be 3 times to our Heavenly Father in thanksgiving for having exalted St. Joseph to a position of such exceptional dignity.)

II

O powerful St. Joseph, you were proclaimed the Patron of the Universal Church, therefore, I invoke you, above all the other Saints, as the greatest protector of the afflicted, and I offer countless blessings to your most generous heart, always ready to help in any need.

To you, O Glorious St. Joseph, come the widows, the orphans, the abandoned, the afflicted, the oppressed. There is no sorrow, heartache or anguish which you has not consoled. I beseech you to use on my behalf those gifts which God has given you, until I too shall be granted the answer to my petition. And you, Holy Souls in Purgatory, pray to St. Joseph for me.

(Recite the Glory Be 3 times to our Heavenly Father in thanksgiving for having exalted St. Joseph to a position of such exceptional dignity.)

III

Countless are those who have prayed to you before me and have received comfort and peace, graces and favors. My heart, so sad and sorrowful, cannot find rest in the midst of this trial which besets me. O Glorious St. Joseph, you know all my needs even before I set them forth in prayer. You know how important this petition is for me. I prostrate myself before you as I sigh under the heavy weight of the problem which confronts me.

There is no human heart in which I can confide my sorrow; and even if I should find a compassionate creature who would be willing to assist me, still he would be unable to help me. Only you can help me in my sorrow, St. Joseph, and I beg you to hear my plea.

Has not St. Theresa left it written in her dialogues that the world may always know "Whatever you ask of St. Joseph, you shall receive."

O St. Joseph, comforter of the afflicted, have pity on my sorrow and pity on those Poor Souls who place so much hope in their prayers to you.

(Recite the Glory Be 3 times to our Heavenly Father in thanksgiving for having exalted St. Joseph to a position of such exceptional dignity.)

IV

O Sublime Patriarch St. Joseph, because of your perfect obedience to God, you may intercede for me.

For your holy life full of grace and merit, hear my prayer.

For your most sweet name, help me. For your most holy tears, comfort me.

For your seven sorrows, intercede for me. For your seven joys, console me.

From all harm of body and soul, deliver me. From all danger and disaster, save me.

Assist me with your powerful intercession and seek for me, through your power and mercy, all that is necessary for my salvation and particularly the favor of which I now stand in such great need.

(Recite the Glory Be 3 times to our Heavenly Father in thanksgiving for having exalted St. Joseph to a position of such exceptional dignity.)

V

O Glorious St. Joseph, countless are the graces and favors which you have obtained for afflicted souls. Illness of every nature, those who are oppressed, persecuted, betrayed, bereft of all human comfort, even those in need of their life bread. All who implore your powerful intercession are comforted in their affliction.

Do not permit, O dearest St. Joseph, that I be the only one of all who has appealed to you, to be denied this petition which I so earnestly beg of you. Show your kindness and generosity even to me, that I may cry out in thanksgiving, "Eternal glory to our Holy Patriarch St. Joseph, my great protector on Earth and the defender of the Holy Souls in Purgatory."

(Recite the Glory Be 3 times to our Heavenly Father in thanksgiving for having exalted St. Joseph to a position of such exceptional dignity.)

VI

Eternal Father, Who art in Heaven, through the merits of Jesus and Mary, I beg You to grant my petition. In the name of Jesus and Mary I prostrate myself before Your Divine presence and I beseech You to accept my hopeful plea to persevere in my prayers that I may be numbered among the throngs of those who live under the patronage of St. Joseph.

Extend Your blessing on this precious treasury of prayers which I today offer to him as a pledge of my devotion.

(Recite the Glory Be 3 times to our Heavenly Father in thanksgiving for having exalted St. Joseph to a position of such exceptional dignity.)

SUPPLICATIONS in honor of St. Joseph's hidden life with JESUS and MARY

St. Joseph, pray that Jesus may come into my soul and sanctify me.

St. Joseph, pray that Jesus may come into my heart and inspire it with charity.

St. Joseph, pray that Jesus may come into my mind and enlighten it.

St. Joseph, pray that Jesus may guide my will and strengthen it.

St. Joseph, pray that Jesus may direct my thoughts and purify them.

St. Joseph, pray that Jesus may guide my desires and direct them.

St. Joseph, pray that Jesus may look upon my deeds and extend His blessings.

St. Joseph, pray that Jesus may inflame me with love for Him.

St. Joseph, request for me from Jesus the imitation of your virtues.

St. Joseph, request for me from Jesus true humility of spirit.

St. Joseph, request for me from Jesus meekness of heart.

St. Joseph, request for me from Jesus peace of soul.

St. Joseph, request for me from Jesus a holy fear of the Lord.

St. Joseph, request for me from Jesus a desire for perfection.

St. Joseph, request for me from Jesus a gentleness of heart.

St. Joseph, request for me from Jesus a pure and charitable heart.

St. Joseph, request for me from Jesus the wisdom of faith.

St. Joseph, request for me from Jesus His blessing of perseverance in my good deeds.

St. Joseph, request for me from Jesus the strength to carry my crosses.

St. Joseph, request for me from Jesus a disdain for the material goods of this world.

St. Joseph, request for me from Jesus the grace to always walk on the narrow path toward Heaven.

St. Joseph, request for me from Jesus the grace to avoid all occasion of sin.

St. Joseph, request for me from Jesus a holy desire for eternal bliss.

St. Joseph, request for me from Jesus the grace of final perseverance.

St. Joseph, do not abandon me.

St. Joseph, pray that my heart may never cease to love you and that my lips may ever praise you.

St. Joseph, for the love you did bear for Jesus, grant that I may learn to love Him.

St. Joseph, graciously accept me as your devoted servant.

St. Joseph, I give myself to you; accept my pleas and hear my prayers.

St. Joseph, do not abandon me at the hour of my death.

Jesus, Mary and Joseph, I give You my heart and my soul.

(Recite the Glory Be 3 times, etc.)

INVOCATIONS TO ST. JOSEPH

I

Remember O most chaste spouse of the Blessed Virgin Mary, my good protector St. Joseph, that never was it known that anyone who came to your protection, and sought your intercession was left unaided. Confidently I prostrate myself before you and fervently beg for your powerful intervention. O foster-Father of our dear Redeemer, despise not my petition, but in your mercy, hear and answer me. Amen.

II

Glorious St. Joseph, spouse of the Blessed Virgin Mary and virginal father of Jesus, look upon me and watch over me; lead me on the path of sanctifying grace; take heed of the urgent needs which I now beg you to envelop within the folds of your fatherly cloak. Dismiss those obstacles and difficulties standing in the way of my prayer and grant that the happy answer to my petition may serve for the greater glory of God and my eternal salvation.

As a pledge of my undying gratitude, I promise to spread the word of your glory whilst offering thanks to the Lord for having so blessed your power and might in Heaven and on earth.

Recite the Litany of St. Joseph:

The Litany of St. Joseph

Lord, have mercy on us.

Christ, have mercy on us.

Lord, have mercy on us. Christ, hear us.

Christ, graciously hear us.

God the Father of Heaven,

Have mercy on us.

God the Son, Redeemer of the world,

Have mercy on us.

God the Holy Spirit,

Have mercy on us.

Holy Trinity, One God,

Have mercy on us.

Holy Mary, pray for us .

St. Joseph, pray for us.

Illustrious son of David,

Light of the patriarchs,

Spouse of the Mother of God,

Chaste guardian of the Virgin,

Foster-father of the Son of God,

Watchful defender of Christ,

Head of the Holy Family,

Joseph most just,

Joseph most chaste,

Joseph most prudent,

Joseph most valiant,

Joseph most obedient,

Joseph most faithful,

Mirror of patience,

Lover of poverty,

Model of workers,

Glory of domestic life,

Guardian of virgins,

Pillar of families,

Solace of the afflicted,

Hope of the sick,

Patron of the dying,

Terror of demons,

Protector of Holy Church,

Lamb of God, Who takes away the sins of the world,

Spare us, O Lord.

Lamb of God, Who takes away the sins of the world,

Graciously hear us, O Lord.

Lamb of God, Who takes away the sins of the world,

Have mercy on us.

V. He made him the lord of His household,
R. And prince over all His possessions.

Let Us Pray.

O God, Who in Thine ineffable providence didst choose Blessed Joseph to be the spouse of Thy most Holy Mother, grant that as we venerate him as our protector on earth, we may deserve to have him as our intercessor in Heaven, Thou Who lives and reigns forever and ever. Amen.

CLOSING PRAYER OF THE HOLY CLOAK

O Glorious Patriarch St. Joseph, you who were chosen by God above all men to be the earthly head of the most holy of families, I beseech you to accept me within the folds of your holy cloak, that you may become the guardian and custodian of my soul.

From this moment on, I choose you as my father, my protector, my counselor, my patron and I beseech you to place in your custody my body, my soul, all that I am, all that I possess, my life and my death.

Look upon me as one of your children; defend me from the treachery of my enemies, invisible or otherwise, assist me at all times in all my necessities; console me in the bitterness of my life, and especially at the hour of my death. Say but one word for me to the Divine Redeemer Whom you were deemed worthy to hold in your arms, and to the Blessed Virgin Mary, your most chase spouse. Request for me those blessings which will lead me to salvation. Include me amongst those who are most dear to you and I shall set forth to prove myself worthy of your special patronage. Amen.

PRAYER TO ST. JOSEPH

To you do we cry in our tribulations, O Blessed St. Joseph, as we confidently invoke your patronage, after that of your most holy spouse, the Blessed Virgin Mary.

By that sacred bond of devotion which linked you to the Immaculate Virgin, Mother of God, and for the fatherly love you did lavish on the child Jesus, we beg you to cast a glance on those heavenly gifts which the Divine Redeemer has obtained for all mankind through His Precious Blood and through your power and mercy, help us in our needs.

O holy protector of the holy family, protect us children of the Lord Jesus Christ; keep far from us the errors and evils which corrupt the world; assist us from Heaven in our struggles against the powers of darkness. And as you once did protect the Divine Child from the cruel edict of Herod, now defend the Church and keep it safe from all dangers and threats; spread over all of us your holy patronage so that by following your example and aided by your spiritual guidance, we may all aspire to a virtuous life, look to a holy death and secure for ourselves the blessing of eternal happiness in Heaven. Amen.

ACKNOWLEDGMENTS

Special thanks for the excellent translation contributions of Hertha Öman, Harriet Krcal, and Jose and Norma Grigio; as well as the excellent editorial contributions of Michael Fontecchio, Bailey Morley, and Christina Martinelli.

ABOUT THE AUTHOR

D r. Mark Miravalle, husband, permanent deacon, and father of eight, earned his doctorate in sacred theology at the Pontifical University of St. Thomas Aquinas in Rome. He has been teaching at the Franciscan University of Steubenville since 1986 and serves as president of the international Catholic movement, *Vox Populi Mariae Mediatrici* (Voice of the People for Mary Mediatrix).

Well known throughout the world for his lectures on Mariology, Dr. Miravalle has addressed several episcopal conferences, including those of South India, Nigeria, Venezuela, and Costa Rica. He has also assisted bishops with preliminary investigations into reported apparitions. Dr. Miravalle has spoken at numerous international conferences and has appeared on EWTN, National Public Radio, BBC, and Fox News. He produces the weekly radio show, "*Mother of All Peoples;* a weekly webcast show, *MaryNow*; a weekly contributor to *Revelant Radio;* is editor of the *Mother of All Peoples* weekly Marian e-Magazine, and is Director of the *International Marian Association.*

Dr. Miravalle is the author and editor of over 20 books in Mariology and Spiritual Theology, including his most recent works, *Meet Your Mother: An Introduction to Mary; Meet Your Spiritual Father: An Introduction to St. Joseph; Time to Meet the Angels,* and *Jesus In You: The Indwelling Trinity in the Souls of the Just.*

51107359R00150

Made in the USA
Middletown, DE
08 November 2017